Contents

Google Maps Mashups with Google Mapplets

By Michael Young

How did it happen so quickly? Since 2005, when Google released its Google Maps API, thousands of applications have been created that let users browse a variety of content (news, images, real estate listings, election results, and so on) using a map. Geographic context, aka maps, provide a powerful and pleasant way to explore and browse many kinds of content.

In July 2007, Google launched Mapplets, which allows developers to create applications that overlay data on maps, similar to the Maps API but with a key difference. Now you can run your own geo-based mashups within Google Maps and make it available to all users of Google Maps (at `http://maps.google.com`*).*

Google Maps Mashups with Google Mapplets is a hands-on guide to creating mashups (combining multiple content sources and services into a single application) with Google Mapplets. This book is split into two parts. The first part covers the basics of Google Mapplets, taking you through simple examples of some of the common Mapplets APIs. The second part shows you how to create a map-based mashup. The book walks you through the steps of creating an application that combines multiple data feeds (Tourfilter concert data), a concert venue search and geocoding API (from Eventful), and the Google Mapplets APIs. In the end, you will have created a mashup that dynamically maps Tourfilter concerts for 60 cities on a Google Mapplet. The basics of data feeds and formats, APIs, and caching are covered—all essential tools when creating mashups.

This book is for developers who want to explore and create geographic-based mashups. The code examples in the book use JavaScript and PHP, so familiarity with both will help. All the server-side examples use PHP, but you can apply the same lessons using other programming languages.

The source code for the book is available on the Apress web site (`http://www.apress.com`*) as well as the author's site at* `http://81nassau.com`*.*

Part 1: Getting Started with Google Mapplets

Chapter 1: Introducing Google Mapplets

When the Google Maps API was released in June 2005, there was an explosion of location-related software development. Craigslist apartment listings, Chicago crime data, Flickr photos, current news events, happy-hour locations, weather, historical sites, public transportation...just about any piece of content imaginable could be overlaid on a map using this API with a little JavaScript.

Fast-forward a few years. So many web sites have a mapping component that at least two sites are dedicated to tracking this phenomenon: Google Maps Mashups (`http://googlemapsmania.blogspot.com`) and Programmable Web (`http://programmableweb.com`). According to Programmable Web, nearly 1,200 of the 1,400 mapping applications are using the Google Maps API—and this is just for the sites Programmable Web is tracking.

In the past, all these map-based applications lived on developer or third-party web sites. However, with the release of Google Mapplets, developers can now create map-based applications (or port their current Google Maps applications) and expose them to every user of Google Maps at `http://maps.google.com`. Google handles the hosting and bandwidth of your application and provides a directory of Mapplets so that users can find your application.

Do I have you on the edge of your seat? Good—let's dive in. In this chapter, you will learn the following:

- The basics of Mapplets
- The developer tools you can use to aid in Mapplet development
- How to write your first Mapplet
- How to use the Google Mapplets APIs to plot data on a map
- The differences between Mapplets and applications based on the standard Google Maps API

What's a Mapplet?

Mapplets are small web applications that run within Google Maps. They are a type of Google Gadget—the framework that allows developers to create small web applications that can run within iGoogle, Google Maps, Orkut, or any web page outside Google. Mapplets use the basic concepts and APIs of Google Gadgets, though they are specifically used within the Google Maps realm.

In its basic form, a Mapplet is an XML file that contains the HTML and JavaScript that make up your application. Mapplets have two components:

- A web application that is displayed on the Google Maps site at `http://maps.google.com`. This application is typically displayed in the lower-left corner of the page on `http://maps.google.com`.

- JavaScript that lets you control the map on `http://maps.google.com`, retrieve external data, or even store and retrieve user preferences.

After you create your Mapplet, it's up to you to host the Mapplet XML file containing your HTML and JavaScript. When a user installs your Mapplet, Google will grab the Mapplet XML file from your server and display it within an `<iframe>` element on `http://maps.google.com`. (An `<iframe>` is an HTML element that is used to embed HTML from another web site in a web page.) In this case, Google uses an `<iframe>` element to embed your Mapplet in `http://maps.google.com`.

Google will cache your Mapplet source and serve it from its own servers at `http://gmodules.com`. This is done for a few reasons:

- To restrict your Mapplet's JavaScript from doing anything harmful such as accessing a user's cookies on `http://maps.google.com`

- To reduce the load on your site from the potential high number of users you'll have

You'll learn more about how to create Mapplets in this chapter, but before you do, let's take a look at a live Mapplet. Open your browser to `http://maps.google.com/`. Click the My Maps tab, and you will see a list of Featured Content along with any maps you have created. Select the one about gas prices, and you'll see a Mapplet in action. Figure 1-1 shows the Gas Prices from GasBuddy.com Mapplet. This Mapplet consists of the application, at the bottom of the left column, and all the map interaction. If the Gas Prices Mapplet is available in your list of featured Mapplets, give it try—enter your ZIP/postal code in the search box, and see what the gas prices are in your area.

Figure 1-1. The Gas Prices from GasBuddy.com Mapplet on http://maps.google.com

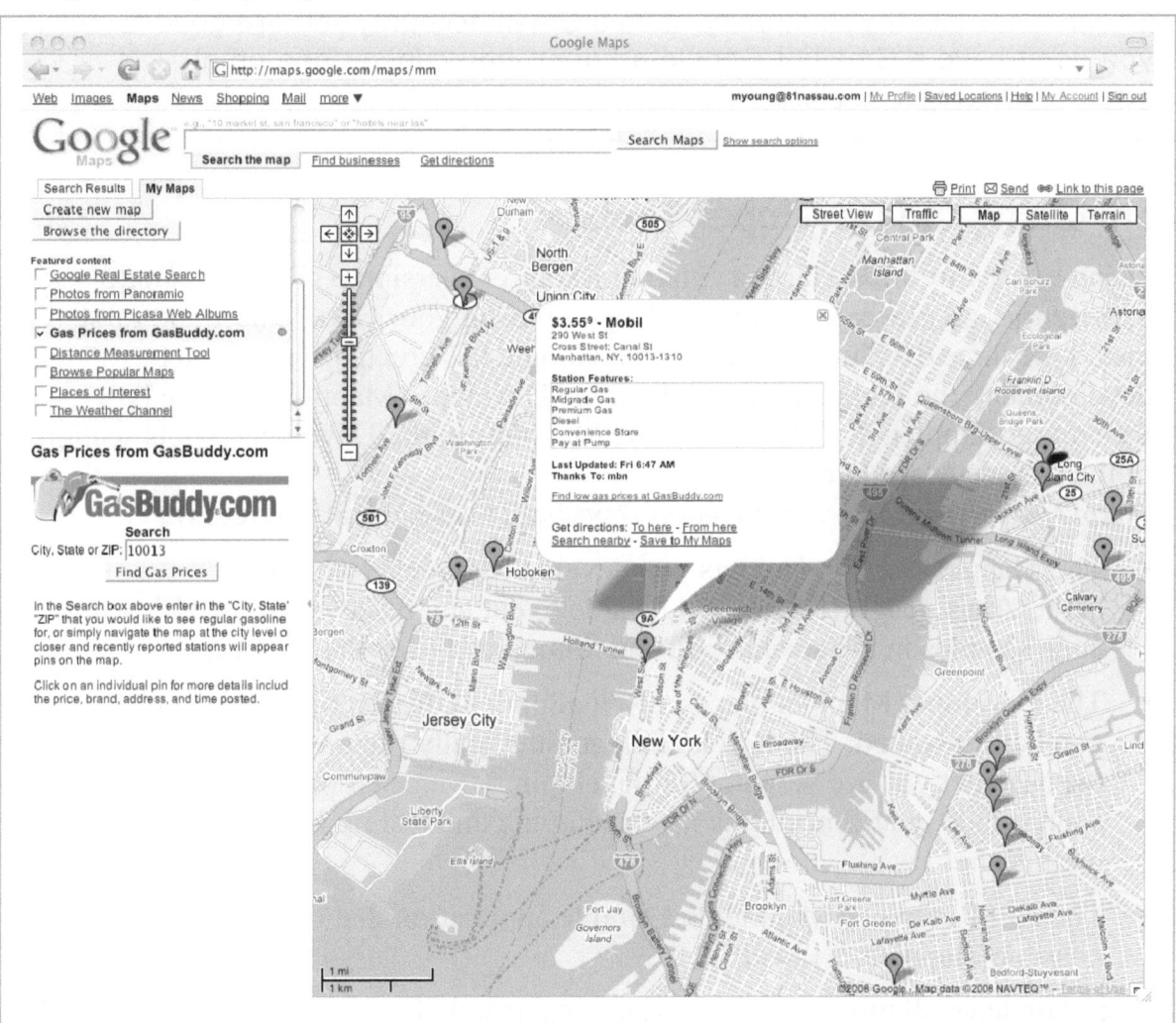

Getting Started with Mapplets

Now that you have a general idea of what a Mapplet is, it's time to roll up your sleeves and start developing. First you'll need to set up your development environment.

Note   Before you can create your first Mapplet, you must have a Google account. If you already have a Gmail account, you are good to go. If you don't have a Gmail or Google account, you can set one up at https://www.google.com/accounts.

Installing the Developer Tools

Using either Firefox, Safari, or Internet Explorer (version 6 or newer), go to http://maps.google.com/maps/mm, and sign in using your Google account. First install the three developer modules that Google has created for Mapplet development: the Mapplet Scratch Pad, the Developer Mapplet, and the API Reference Mapplet. You can find these Mapplets in the Developer Tools section of the Google Maps Directory (http://maps.google.com/ig/directory?synd=mpl&pid=mpl&cat=devtools).

- The Mapplet Scratch Pad lets you develop Mapplets right in http://maps.google.com. You'll be able to cut and paste all of the following code samples in the scratch pad and immediately see the application.

- The Developer Mapplet places a Reload link at the top of each Mapplet that you have installed. The Reload link automatically reloads the source code for the Mapplet you are viewing (or developing). Since Google caches Mapplet source code, you'll need this for developing and testing Mapplets. Trust me on this one!

- The API Reference Mapplet is a simple application that displays all the possible Mapplets API calls.

Once you have all three developer Mapplets installed, select the Mapplet Scratch Pad. Your maps.google.com page should now look like Figure 1-2.

Figure 1-2. Developer Mapplets installed on the My Maps tab

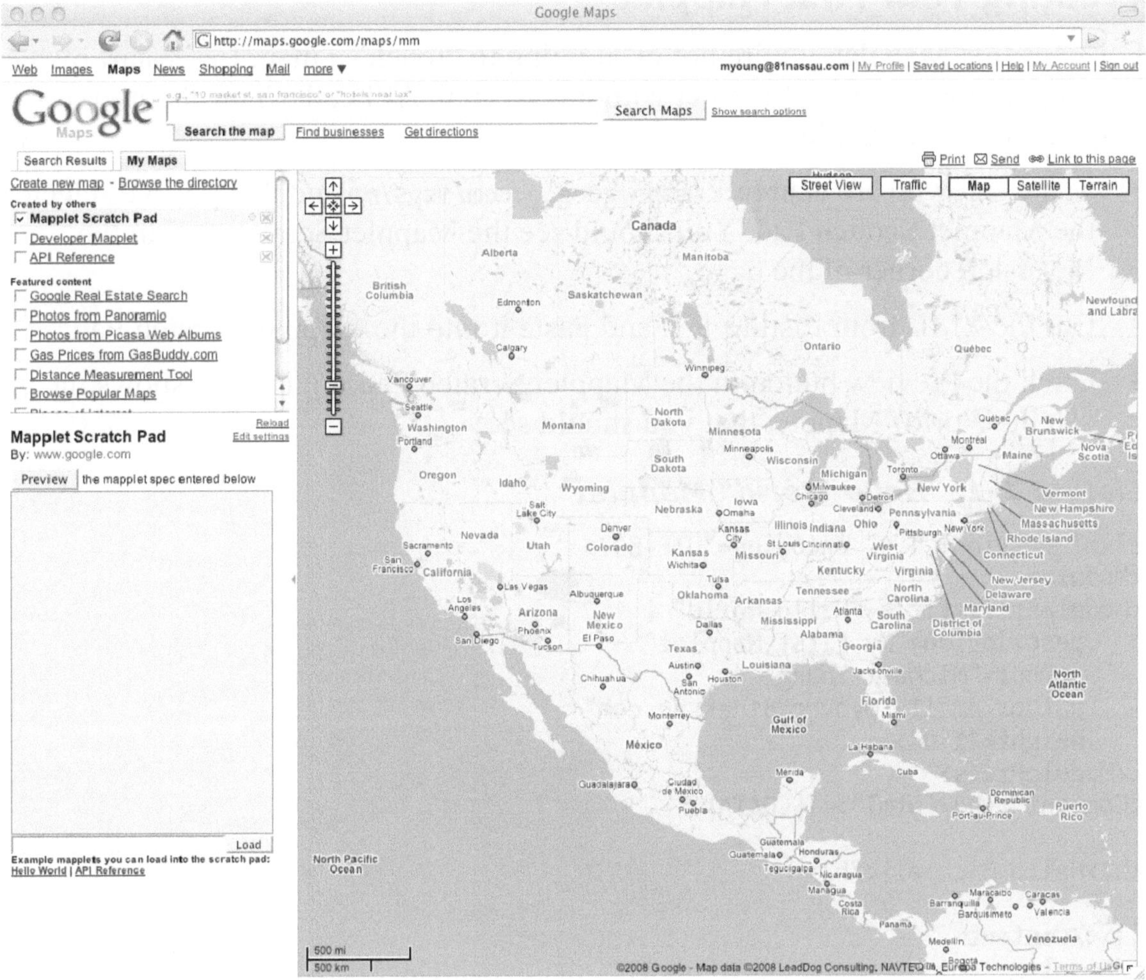

Creating Your First Mapplet

For your first Mapplet, you're not even going to "touch" a map. Let's start by creating a simple "shell" Mapplet without any map API calls. You'll get to the map in the next example.

- Make sure you are at **http://maps.google.com/maps/mm** and that you've selected the Mapplet Scratch Pad. You should see the Mapplet Scratch Pad in the lower-left corner of the page.

- Cut the XML from Listing 1-1, and paste it into the Mapplet Scratch Pad.

- Click the Preview button in the Mapplet Scratch Pad. Figure 1-3 shows the "Hello World" Mapplet that you should see.

Listing 1-1. "Hello World" Mapplet

```
<?xml version="1.0" encoding="UTF-8"?>
<Module>
<ModulePrefs title="Hello World"
    description="My First Mapplet"
    author="Michael Young"
    author_email="myoung@81nassau.com"
    height="150">
</ModulePrefs>
<Content type="html"><![CDATA[

<h2>Hello Michael!</h2>

]]></Content>
</Module>
```

Figure 1-3. The "Hello World" Mapplet in Firefox

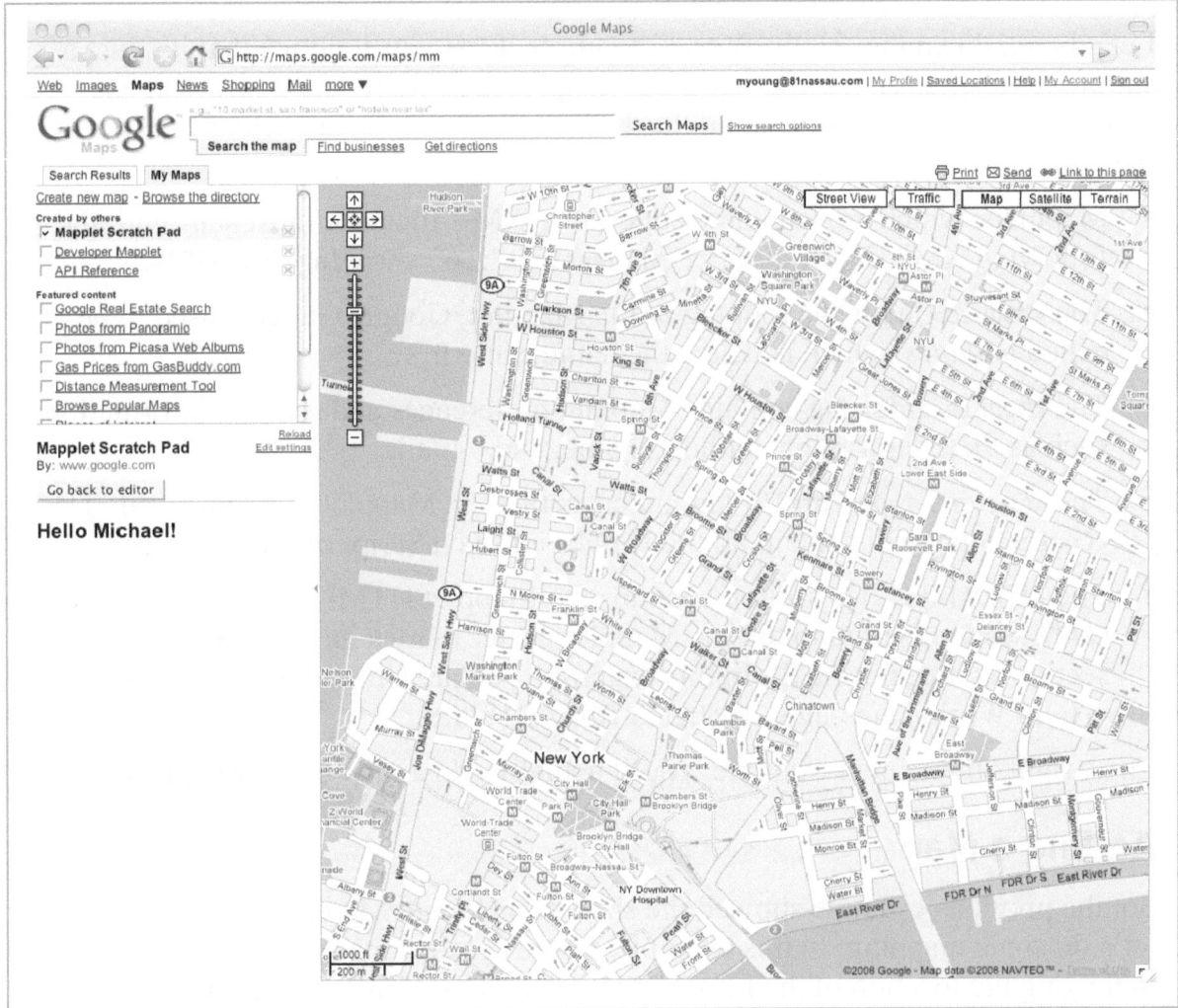

Examining the Code

Let's break down the "Hello World" example. First you'll notice that it's just a simple XML file. This is the standard Mapplet shell XML file that you'll use with most of the Mapplet code in this book. Here is a look at each of the tags in the XML file:

- Mapplets, which are Google Gadgets, are XML files and must start with the following XML declaration: `<?xml version="1.0" encoding="UTF-8"?>`.

- The `<Module>` tag is the root tag of the Mapplet. Google Gadgets used to be called *modules*, which is where the name came from.

- The `<ModulePrefs>` tag contains Mapplet preferences and settings information, such as title, description, author's name, and e-mail.

- The `<Content type="html">` tag indicates that the Mapplet is of type `html`. The `<Content>` tag will contain all the HTML and JavaScript of the Mapplet.

- The `<![CDATA[...]]>` section contains the Mapplet HTML and JavaScript. The `CDATA` section is used to tell the Mapplet parser to treat anything inside the section as text, not XML. In this example, you are simply displaying the "Hello World" message: `<h2>Hello Michael!</h2>`.

Easy, right? In the next example, you'll actually add a map to your application.

Adding a Map

So, the previous example showed the shell of a Google Mapplet/Gadget. Now let's do some mapping. In this example, you'll create a map and add a marker indicating the location of the Empire State Building. You'll also center the map on this point.

1. In the Mapplet Scratch Pad, click the "Go back to editor" button to display the scratch pad editor.

2. Cut the XML from Listing 1-2, and paste it into the Mapplet Scratch Pad.

3. Click the Preview button in the Mapplet Scratch Pad. You should see the Mapplet shown in Figure 1-4.

Listing 1-2. Create a Map and Add a Marker to the Map

```xml
<?xml version="1.0" encoding="UTF-8"?>
<Module>
<ModulePrefs title="Empire State Building"
    description="Creating a Simple Map and Marker"
    author="Michael Young"
    author_email="myoung@81nassau.com"
    height="150">
<Require feature="sharedmap"/>
</ModulePrefs>
<Content type="html"><![CDATA[

<h2>Empire State Building</h2>

<script>

    // Create a map and center it over the Empire State Building
    var map = new GMap2();
    var point = new GLatLng(40.748330, -73.984615);
    map.setCenter(point, 17);

    // Add a marker right on the Empire State Building
    var marker = new GMarker(point);
    map.addOverlay(marker);

</script>

]]></Content>
</Module>
```

Figure 1-4. Empire State Building Mapplet in Firefox

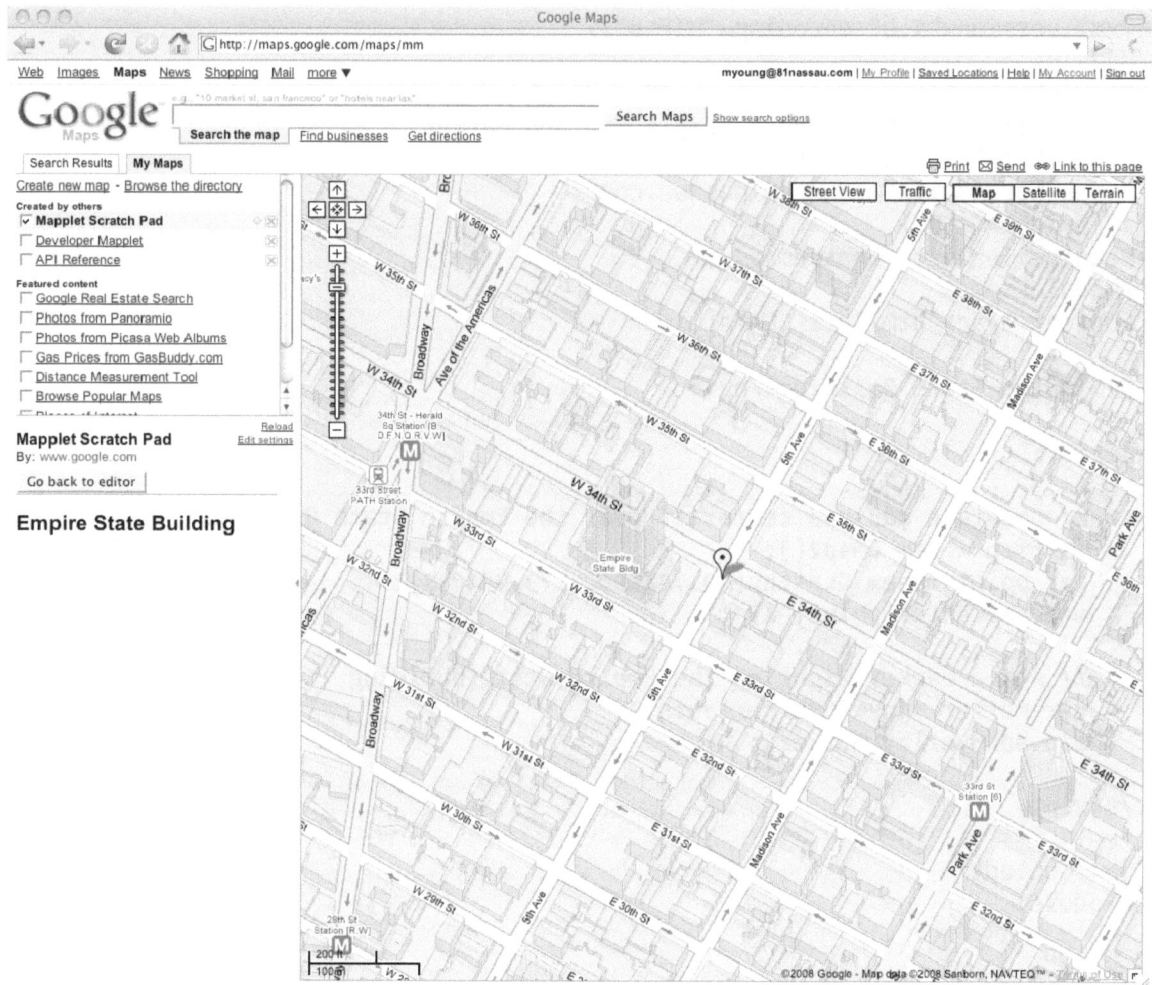

Examining the Code

Congratulations, you've created your first, er, second, Mapplet! Go ahead, pat yourself on the back. I can wait. OK, good, now let's take a look at the code to see what's new in this one.

First, and most important, you added `<Require feature="sharedmap"/>` to the `<ModulePrefs>` tag. By adding this tag, the Mapplet JavaScript is loaded so that your Mapplet can control the map.

Tip To load the Mapplets API, add the `<Require feature="sharedmap"/>` tag inside the `<ModulePrefs>` tag of your Mapplet XML file.

Next, inside the `<Content>` section, where the main application code resides, you added some JavaScript inside a `<script>` tag. This is where all the JavaScript that communicates with the map resides.

This example has introduced three Google Maps API classes: `GMap2`, `GLatLng`, and `GMarker`. Let's talk through each of these line by line.

The first line of code creates an instance of the `GMap2` class and assigns it to the variable `map`. The `map` variable is now a reference to the map on `http://maps.google.com`.

```
var map = new GMap2();
```

Now that you can control the map, center it over the Empire State Building in New York. To center the map, you need to specify the latitude and longitude of the center point—the Empire State Building in this case. You can create a point using the `GLatLng` class:

```
var point = new GLatLng(40.748330, -73.984615);
```

To create a point using the `GLatLng` class, you need to pass in two arguments: the latitude and longitude of the point you want to create. So, you've passed in the latitude 40.748330 and the longitude –73.984615, which happens to be the latitude/longitude of the Empire State Building.

GEOCODING: CONVERTING ADDRESSES TO LATITUDE AND LONGITUDE

Geocoding is the process of converting a location into a latitude and longitude pair. *Location* in this case can refer to a country, city, street, or address. For example, the address of the Empire State Building—350 5th Avenue, New York, NY—has a latitude of 40.748330 and a longitude of −73.984615.

Throughout the book, you will be converting addresses to latitude and longitude so that you can place locations on the map. You'll notice that many of the Mapplets API calls, such as creating a point and placing an info window on the map, require you to know the latitude and longitude of the location.

You can find many geocoding services on the Web to help you convert addresses to latitude and longitude. Google even has a Geocoding API so that you can create your own geocode tools. For the examples in this chapter, I'm using a simple tool that I built using the Google Maps and Geocode APIs, which will display the latitude and longitude of an address. You can find the tool here: **http://81nassau.com/demos/geocode/**.

Now that you have your point, you can center the map using the **setCenter()** method. The **setCenter()** method takes two arguments: the point where you want to center the map and the zoom level:

```
map.setCenter(point, 17);
```

Finally, you place a marker on the map right on the Empire State Building. The marker code is pretty simple. Just create a new **GMarker** object, and add it to the map using the **addOverlay()** map method. To create the **GMarker**, you'll need to pass in the point object (**GLatLng**) you created earlier.

```
var marker = new GMarker(point);
map.addOverlay(marker);
```

Not too bad, right? In one example, you learned how to create a marker and center the map.

Adding an Info Window

The previous example put a marker on the map, but it didn't really tell you much. If you're placing a marker on the map, it would be nice for the marker to tell what it's pointing at, right? Fortunately, the Google Mapplets API lets you display an info window on the map. You can create as many info windows as you want, but you can show only one info window at a time. Let's modify the previous example to display an info window above the maker on the Empire State Building when the map first loads.

An info window can display HTML and CSS but for security reasons cannot contain JavaScript. You can find a list of the HTML and CSS allowed in info windows at **http://www.google.com/apis/maps/documentation/mapplets/ infowindowallowed.html**.

1. In the Mapplet Scratch Pad, click the "Go back to editor" button to display the scratch pad editor.

2. Cut the XML from Listing 1-3, and paste it into the Mapplet Scratch Pad.

3. Click the Preview button in the scratch pad. You should see the Mapplet shown in Figure 1-5.

Listing 1-3. Add an Info Window Above the Empire State Building Marker

```
<?xml version="1.0" encoding="UTF-8"?>
<Module>
<ModulePrefs title="Empire State Building"
    description="Adding an Info Window to our Map"
    author="Michael Young"
    author_email="myoung@81nassau.com"
    height="150">
<Require feature="sharedmap"/>
</ModulePrefs>
<Content type="html"><![CDATA[

<h2>Empire State Building</h2>

<script>
```

```
// Create a map and center it over the Empire State Building
var map = new GMap2();
var point = new GLatLng(40.748330, -73.984615);
map.setCenter(point, 17);

// Add a marker right on the Empire State Building
var marker = new GMarker(point);
map.addOverlay(marker);

// Open an Info Window
var info = "<h2>Empire State Building</h2>";
marker.openInfoWindow(info);

</script>

]]></Content>
</Module>
```

Figure 1-5. Info window above the Empire State Building

Examining the Code

In this example, you just added a single line of code to display an info window above the marker that you created marking the location of the Empire State Building:

```
marker.openInfoWindow(info);
```

`openInfoWindow()` takes an HTML DOM element as an argument. In this case, you're displaying "Empire State Building" in bold text. The HTML is displayed over the marker when the map loads.

Making the Marker Clickable

In the previous example, you displayed the info window above your marker as soon as the map loaded. Let's take that a step further by adding multiple markers to the map and an info window that displays when a user clicks the marker. The Mapplets API provides a simple method to display an info window when a marker is clicked.

Please note that I'm moving on from the Empire State Building example. You're working your way toward a mashup where you are going to map various bars, clubs, and venues. In this next example, you'll add a few New York clubs to the map, the Knitting Factory and the Bowery Ballroom:

1.   In the Mapplet Scratch Pad, click the "Go back to editor" button to display the scratch pad editor.

2.   Cut the XML from Listing 1-4, and paste it into the Mapplet Scratch Pad.

3.   Click the Preview button in the scratch pad. You should see the Mapplet shown in Figure 1-6.

Listing 1-4. Display the Info Window When Each Marker Is Clicked

```
<?xml version="1.0" encoding="UTF-8"?>
<Module>
<ModulePrefs title="New York Clubs"
    description="Adding Clickable Info Windows to Our Map"
    author="Michael Young"
    author_email="myoung@81nassau.com"
```

```
    height="150">
<Require feature="sharedmap"/>
</ModulePrefs>
<Content type="html"><![CDATA[

<h2>New York Clubs</h2>

<script>

    // Create a map
    var map = new GMap2();

    // Create two points and markers:
    // One for the Knitting Factory and one for the Bowery Ballroom
    var pointKF = new GLatLng(40.7173, -74.0053);
    var pointBB = new GLatLng(40.7205, -73.9937);

    // Now create the markers
    var markerKF = new GMarker(pointKF, {title: "Knitting Factory"});
    var markerBB = new GMarker(pointBB, {title: "Bowery Ballroom"});

    markerKF.bindInfoWindow("<h2>Knitting Factory</h2>");
    markerBB.bindInfoWindow("<h2>Bowery Ballroom</h2>");

    // Add the markers to the map
    map.addOverlay(markerKF);
    map.addOverlay(markerBB);

    // Center the map over Manhattan so we can see both markers
    map.setCenter(new GLatLng(40.7204, -73.9998), 15);

</script>

]]></Content>
</Module>
```

Figure 1-6. The marker's info window is displayed when clicked.

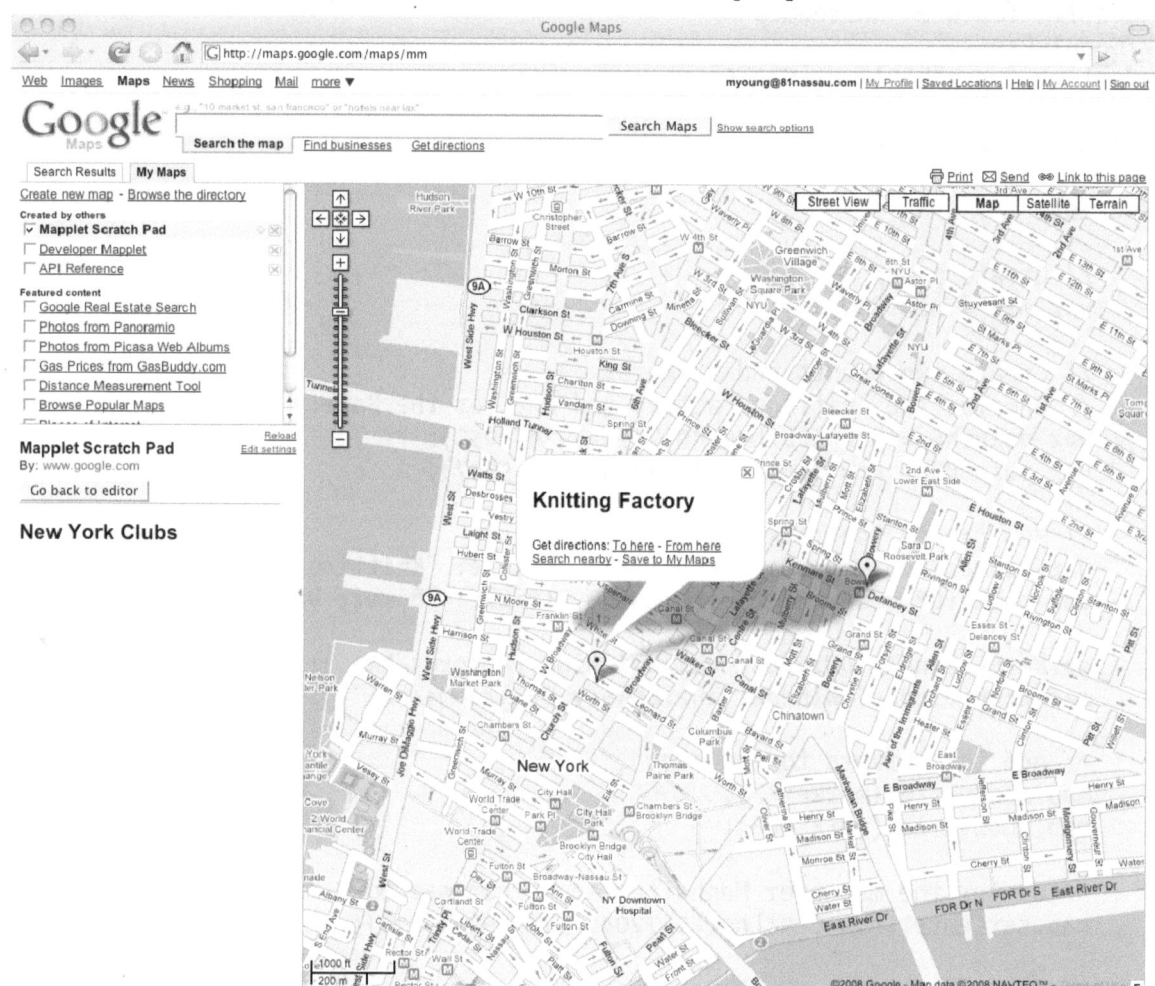

Examining the Code

To make things more interesting, you added two markers to the map: one above the Knitting Factory and one above the Bowery Ballroom. The special sauce in this example is the `bindInfoWindow()` method, which tells the map to display the info window whenever the marker is clicked.

Responding to Mapplet Events

The Mapplets API includes functions that allow you to respond to user interactions with the map, such as moving the map or clicking a marker. When an interaction occurs, say a user clicking a marker, a JavaScript event is triggered. The Mapplets API allows you to respond to these events, adding any custom behavior you want after receiving the event. In this example, you'll take a look at how to display an info window after a marker is clicked. This example is functionally the same as the previous example in Listing 1-4, but you'll respond directly to the "click" event in this example.

1. In the Mapplet Scratch Pad, click the "Go back to editor" button to display the scratch pad editor.

2. Cut the XML from Listing 1-5, and paste it into the Mapplet Scratch Pad.

3. Click the Preview button in the scratch pad. You should see the Mapplet shown in Figure 1-7.

Listing 1-5. Display the Info Window When Each Marker Is Clicked

```
<?xml version="1.0" encoding="UTF-8"?>
<Module>
<ModulePrefs title="New York Clubs"
    description="Responding to Mapplet Events"
    author="Michael Young"
    author_email="myoung@81nassau.com"
    height="150">
<Require feature="sharedmap"/>
</ModulePrefs>
<Content type="html"><![CDATA[

<h2>New York Clubs</h2>

<script>

    function createMarker(point, venue) {
        var marker = new GMarker(point, {title: venue});

        GEvent.addListener(marker, "click", function() {
            var html  = "<b>" + venue + "</b>";
```

```
            marker.openInfoWindowHtml(html);
        });
        return marker;
    }

    // Create a map
    var map = new GMap2();

    // Create two points and markers:
    // One for the Knitting Factory and one for the Bowery Ballroom
    var pointKF = new GLatLng(40.7173, -74.0053);
    var pointBB = new GLatLng(40.7205, -73.9937);

    // Now create the markers
    var markerKF = createMarker(pointKF, "Knitting Factory");
    var markerBB = createMarker(pointBB, "Bowery Ballroom");

    // Add the markers to the map
    map.addOverlay(markerKF);
    map.addOverlay(markerBB);

    // Center the map over Manhattan so we can see both markers
    map.setCenter(new GLatLng(40.7204, -73.9998), 15);

</script>

]]></Content>
</Module>
```

Figure 1-7. The marker's info window is displayed when clicked.

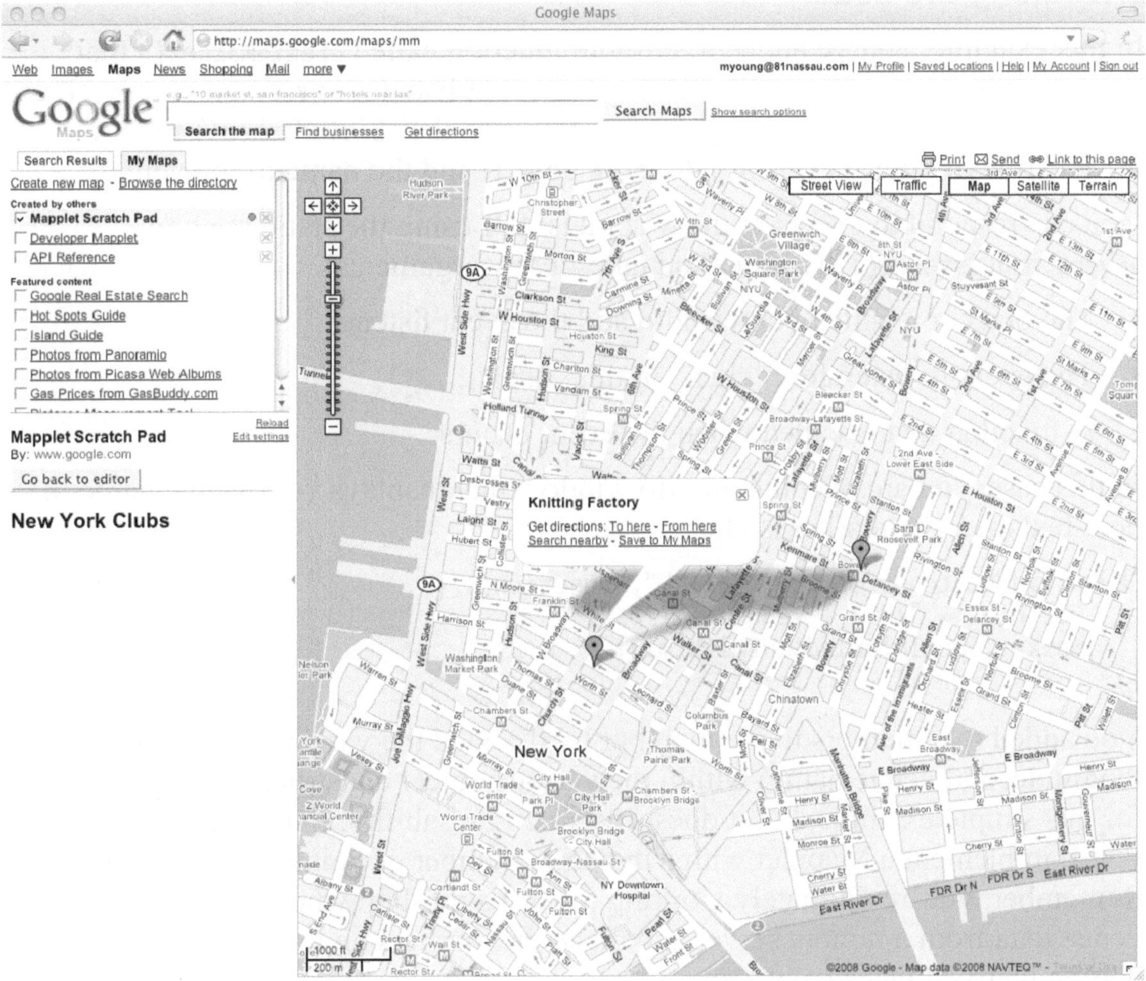

Examining the Code

In this example, you've added a reusable function called **createMarker()** that creates your marker for you and adds your event listener to respond to any clicks on the marker. The arguments you are passing to the **createMarker()** function are the location of your maker (as a **GLatLng** object) and the name of the venue.

You can respond to events in the Mapplets API using the static method **GEvent.addListener()**. This method takes a few arguments:

- The object on which you want to add the event listener
- The event to listen for ("click" in this case)
- A function that is called when the event occurs

In this case, you are opening an info window that displays your venue name in bold text after the marker is clicked:

```
GEvent.addListener(marker, "click", function() {
    var html = "<b>" + venue + "</b>";
    marker.openInfoWindowHtml(html);
});
```

You added two markers to the map but hard-coded the variables (latitude, longitude, and venue name) within the various object constructors. This is fine for this simple example, but it doesn't scream reusability. In the next example, you'll implement a Mapplet with a dynamic number of points and markers. Remember, you're ultimately working toward a mashup where you will pull the venue data from a remote server and place the markers on the map. You're getting there...it takes baby steps.

I have one more thing to mention here: the last line of this example centered the map using a latitude and longitude pair over downtown Manhattan that I picked because it looked like it was somewhere between the two venue markers:

```
map.setCenter(new GLatLng(40.7204, -73.9998), 15);
```

In the next example, you'll see how to center and scale the map dynamically based on all the markers you have on the map so that you can see all of them on the map at one time.

Using Dynamic Markers and Setting Map Bounds

In this example, you'll clean up the previous example by dynamically adding markers to the map. Instead of hard-coding the data such as latitude, longitude, and info window text in your Mapplet, you will ultimately retrieve this data from an external data source. In the next chapter, you'll learn how to retrieve this data from an external server/database, but for now you'll use data structures to store the data.

Since you have multiple markers that you want to create on the map, you'll need to store the data in a JavaScript array. Arrays in JavaScript look like this:

```
var venues = [ 'Knitting Factory', 'Bowery Ballroom', 'Warsaw' ];
```

This is a start, but it gets you only so far. You really need to store more than just the venue name; you also need the latitude and longitude of the venue. Enter JavaScript *objects*. Objects essentially let you store any combination of name/value pairs and look like this:

```
var marker = ↪
{ "venue": "Knitting Factory",  "lat": 40.7173, "lng": -74.0053 };
```

OK, now you're getting closer. The object lets you store all the needed data for a single venue: the venue name, the latitude, and the longitude. Now you can just store multiple objects in an array, and you're set:

```
var data = [
        { "venue": "Knitting Factory",  "lat": 40.7173, "lng": -74.0053},
        { "venue": "Bowery Ballroom", "lat": 40.7205, "lng": -73.9937}
    ];
```

You'll see in the following example how easy it is to *iterate* (loop) over the data array. You can use the JavaScript **for** loop to accomplish this:

```
var count = data.length;

for (var i = 0; i < count; i++) {
    // create the marker and place it on the map
    var club = data[i];
    // club now contains one of our club/venue objects
}
```

This example had also introduced some new code that will help center the map and set its zoom level so that you can see all your markers on the map when the map first loads. You had to hard-code the center point and zoom level in the previous examples, and now you can do it dynamically. I'll talk more about how you do that after you run through the example.

1. In the Mapplet Scratch Pad, click the "Go back to editor" button to display the scratch pad editor.

2. Cut the XML from Listing 1-6, and paste it into the Mapplet Scratch Pad.

3. Click the Preview button in the scratch pad. You should see the Mapplet shown in Figure 1-8.

Listing 1-6. Creating Dynamic Markers on the Map

```xml
<?xml version="1.0" encoding="UTF-8"?>
<Module>
<ModulePrefs title="New York Clubs"
    description="Dynamically Adding Clickable Markers to the Map"
    author="Michael Young"
    author_email="myoung@81nassau.com"
    height="150">
<Require feature="sharedmap"/>
</ModulePrefs>
<Content type="html"><![CDATA[

<h2>New York Clubs</h2>

<script>

    function createMarker(point, venue) {
        var marker = new GMarker(point, {title: venue});

        GEvent.addListener(marker, "click", function() {
            var html  = "<b>" + venue + "</b>";
            marker.openInfoWindowHtml(html);
        });
        return marker;
    }
```

```
var data = [
    { "venue": "Knitting Factory", "lat": 40.7173, "lng": -74.0053},
    { "venue": "Bowery Ballroom",  "lat": 40.7205, "lng": -73.9937}
];

// Create a map
var map    = new GMap2();
var bounds = new GLatLngBounds();

var count = data.length;
for (var i = 0; i < count; i++) {
    var club = data[i];

    // Add the marker to the map
    var point  = new GLatLng(club.lat, club.lng);
    map.addOverlay(createMarker(point, club.venue));

    // Add the point to our bounds object
    bounds.extend(point);
}

// Find the proper zoom level for the bounds and center the map
map.getBoundsZoomLevelAsync(bounds, function(level) {
    map.setCenter(bounds.getCenter());
    map.setZoom(level);
});

</script>

]]></Content>
</Module>
```

Figure 1-8. The two clubs are shown at the proper zoom level.

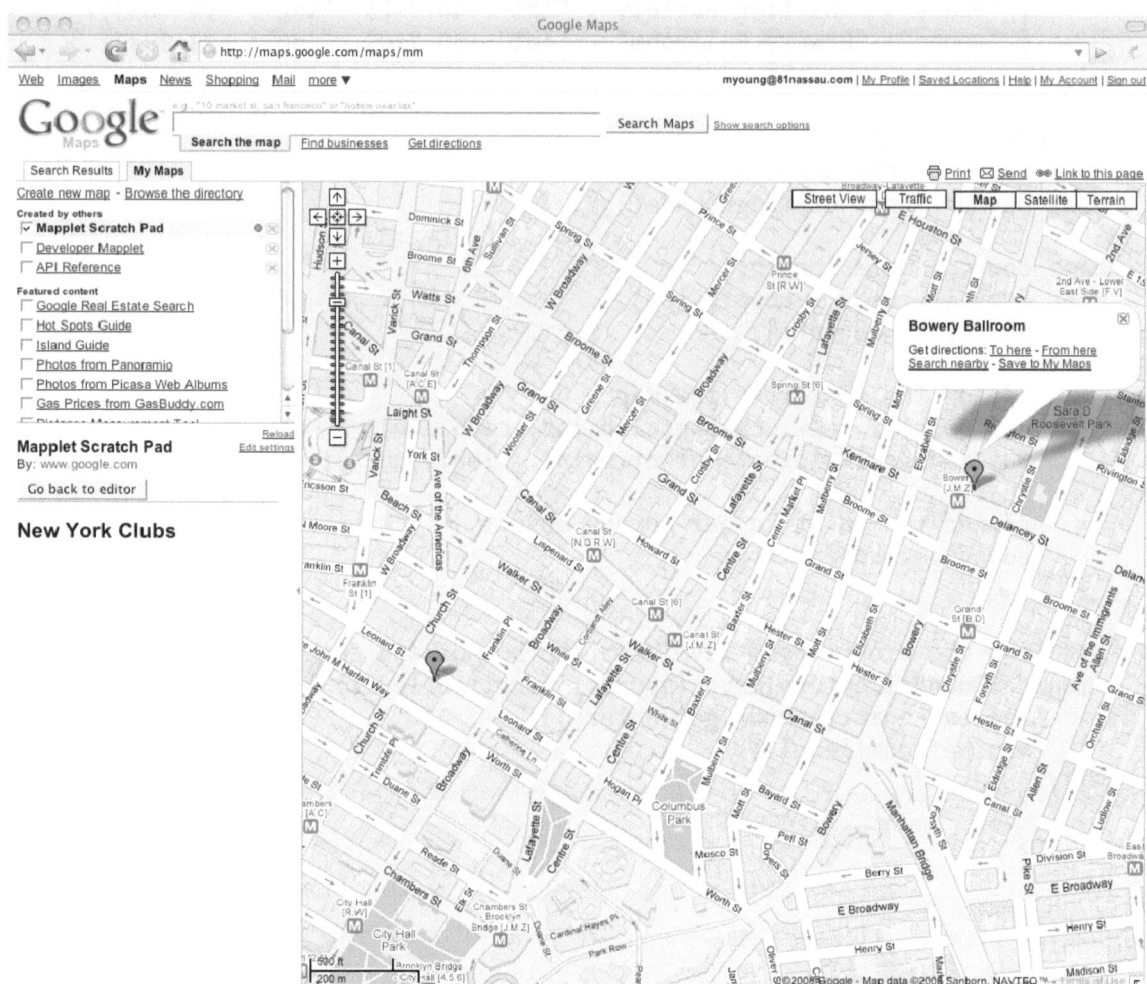

Examining the Code

A lot is going on in this example. First, you're using an array to store your venue data so you can create a dynamic number of markers on your map:

```
var data = [
    { "venue": "Knitting Factory",  "lat": 40.7173, "lng": -74.0053},
    { "venue": "Bowery Ballroom", "lat": 40.7205, "lng": -73.9937},
];
```

After creating the map, you loop over the data array using a **for** loop, extracting the venue name, latitude, and longitude for each venue and creating a **GLatLng** and a **GMarker** for each venue:

```
var count = data.length;
for (var i = 0; i < count; i++) {
    var club = data[i];

    // Add the marker to the map
    var point  = new GLatLng(club.lat, club.lng);
    map.addOverlay(createMarker(point, club.venue));
    //...
}
```

Remember that the **data** array is storing JavaScript objects. The line **var club = data[i];** will give you a single object from the **data** array. Now that you have an object stored in the variable **club**, you can extract the individual fields like this: **club["lat"]** or **club.lat**.

Also notice in this example that you are using the new Mapplet class **GLatLngBounds**. This class will ultimately help you center the map so that you can view all the markers on the map when the application first loads. The **GLatLngBounds** object will store all the **GLatLng** points you create, representing the boundary of all the points that you "add" to the **bounds** object. You add a point to the **bounds** object with the following code:

```
bounds.extend(point);
```

After the **for** loop completes and has added all the points on the map to the **GLatLngBounds** object, you need to set the map's center point and zoom level so that the view scales to display all the markers. You can use the **GMap2** method **getBoundsZoomLevelAsync()** to help you with this. To get the proper zoom level for your **GLatLngBounds** object, you call **getBoundsZoomLevelAsync()** with two arguments: the **GLatLngBounds** object and a callback function. You need the callback here because the **getBoundsZoomLevel** method is asynchronous—notice the **Async** at the end of the method name. This means that when you call the method, the Mapplets API will return the proper zoom level once the map responds. So in this case, the callback function will receive the proper map zoom level, and inside the callback, you can set the map's zoom level and center point:

```
map.getBoundsZoomLevelAsync(bounds, function(level) {
    map.setCenter(bounds.getCenter());
    map.setZoom(level);
});
```

How Mapplets Differ from Standard Google Maps

Google Mapplets API calls are based on the standard Google Maps API, but a few differences are worthy of mention. The following sections illustrate the most important differences between Mapplets and standard Google Maps:

- API initialization

- Requesting data from remote servers

- Communication between your application and the map

- Info window restrictions

The Mapplet main documentation page (`http://www.google.com/apis/maps/ documentation/mapplets/guide.html`) includes a complete list of differences.

Easy API Initialization

Initializing the Maps API is a bit easier in Mapplets than with standard Google Maps. You can skip a few steps when creating a Mapplet:

- With Google Maps, you need to register your application and obtain an API key before you can get started. The API key is necessary when loading the Google Maps JavaScript library from your application. With Mapplets, you don't need an API key to get started.

- You don't need to manually load the Google Maps API JavaScript library. Including the `<Require feature="sharedmap"/>` tag in your Mapplet will automatically load the library for you.

- You create a map with the `GMap2` class. With Google Maps, you need to pass the `<div>` element of your map to the `GMap2` constructor:

  ```
  var map = new GMap2(document.getElementById("map"));
  ```

- This isn't needed in Mapplets, because the constructor will return a reference to the map on **maps.google.com**:

  ```
  var map = new GMap2();
  ```

- You don't need to check whether the browser that loads your Mapplet is compatible with Google Maps. You can assume that your Mapplet's users have a compatible browser. In fact, the **GBrowserIsCompatible** check is not supported in Mapplets since you will never need to check for browser compatibility.

- Setting the initial position of the map via **setCenter()** is not required. You can certainly center the map using this method, but the map is already centered for you over your country of residence by default.

Requesting Data from Remote Servers

Web browsers have a built-in security feature that allows JavaScript to access XML data only from the same domain from which it was served. For example, if you have a web page that was served from **http://www.nytimes.com**, you can't use JavaScript in that web page to fetch XML from **http://www.google.com**. This security feature is typically called the *same origin policy* and protects your application from loading data from a web site that isn't trusted.

Note   The *same origin policy* is a JavaScript security policy built in to all web browsers. This prevents scripts from one web site from accessing potentially harmful data from another site.

Mapplets are served from a Google domain (**gmodules.com**), so you cannot use the standard Google Maps API calls **GDownloadURL** or **GXml** to request remote data. These API calls can download data only from the web server (domain) that served the application, which in this case is **http://gmodules.com**.

To request remote data from a Mapplet, use either **_IG_FetchContent()** or **_IG_FetchXmlContent()**. **_IG_FetchContent()** will fetch both text and HTML, and **_IG_FetchXmlContent()** will fetch XML data. Both of these APIs act as proxies, so you can fetch data from your own web server as well as from other remote servers. Google will also cache the content you retrieve using these APIs in order to reduce the load on the remote servers.

Communicating Between Your Application and the Map

Since communication between a Mapplet and the map is asynchronous, you will need to use callbacks to obtain the value returned from some Mapplets API calls. All Mapplets APIs that require callbacks have **Async** appended to the name of the API call. Google Maps API calls, on the other hand, are synchronous, returning immediately after the call is made.

For example, with the standard Google Maps, you can obtain the latitude and longitude of the center of the map with the following example:

```
// get the lat/lng of the center of the map
var center = map.getCenter();
alert("center: " + center.lat() + ", " + center.lng());
```

Getting the latitude and longitude of the center of the map in a Mapplet is slightly different. Remember that with the asynchronous communication, the result (the center of the map in this case) may not be returned immediately.

```
// get the lat/lng of the center of the map (Mapplet)
map.getCenterAsync(function(center) {
    alert("center: " + center.lat() + ", " + center.lng());
});
// you will reach this point in the code before you get the map's center
```

Info Window Restrictions

As mentioned earlier, Mapplets are served from the Google domain `gmodules.com` and run within an `<iframe>` element. This is done so that a Mapplet's JavaScript doesn't do anything harmful (such as access a Google user's cookies). It's not that they don't trust your Mapplet—it's the shady guy's Mapplet they don't trust!

Everything map related, including the info windows, is served from `http://maps.google.com`. So, to protect itself from any harmful JavaScript running on the map, Google does not allow any JavaScript in the info windows. In the same vein, Google permits only a subset of HTML and CSS in your info windows. For example, the CSS properties `expression()` and `background-image` are not allowed. For the complete list of allowed HTML and CSS, please visit `http://www.google.com/apis/maps/documentation/mapplets/infowindowallowed.html`

Summary

Congratulations! I hope you've come this far unscarred. This chapter covered a lot, and more good things are coming. You now have an introduction to the Mapplets API and can plot markers on the map and respond to some basic map events such as marker clicks. This is a great start!

In the next chapter, you'll learn how to load map data from remote servers. This is when the code starts to get interesting.

Chapter 2: Using Remote Data in Your Mapplets

You now have Mapplet basics down. In the previous chapter, you learned how to plot markers on a map using *static* content, or content that never changes. It is now time to make your application more interactive by using *dynamic* data, or data that is retrieved from remote servers.

Mapping data sets that don't often change (if ever), such as a chain store's locations or a series of historical buildings, may not require dynamic retrieval. However, when you start to map information that changes often, such as news or event data (like concerts), you'll need to periodically retrieve the data to refresh your application. In this chapter, you'll learn how to do just that.

Specifically, you will explore the following:

- Typical data formats used in data feeds and web services
- Google's JavaScript APIs to fetch remote content
- Techniques for making Mapplets more interactive and responsive
- Tools for plotting dynamic content with Mapplets

Data Feed Formats

Before you get started retrieving remote content, I'll discuss the data formats. You'll see plenty of acronyms for data formats: CSV, XML, RSS, Atom, KML, JSON…. These are a few of the popular flavors of the moment, and you might retrieve any of them from a remote server or with a web service. The following sections highlight the ones you'll be using in this book.

CSV: The Equivalent of Cave Paintings

Comma-separated values (CSV) is an ancient file format that you've most likely encountered as an export type for spreadsheets and flat-file databases. It is a plain-text data format that uses commas to delimit simple fields in a text file.

It's worth a mention, though it's not as commonly used on the Web as some of the other formats mentioned next. You can imagine the fields in a data file that you'd need to store some mapping/marker information: the marker description (in this case, the band and venue name), the latitude, and the longitude. Data in a CSV file looks like this:

```
 the redwalls, Knitting Factory, 40.7173, -74.0053, ↦
dirty projectors, Bowery Ballroom, 40.7205, -73.9937
```

XML: The Worldwide Format

Many publishing and data feed formats are based on Extensible Markup Language (XML), including RSS, Atom, KML, and so on. Most data feeds on the Internet today are some flavor of XML. All modern browsers have built-in support for parsing XML data using JavaScript APIs.

Note   You can find more information about XML at the W3C: http://www.w3.org/XML/.

You'll be using XML with most of the examples in this book, so let's look at a simple XML file that stores the sample marker data, as in the previous example. This is some simple XML that you can use to store concert data:

```
<?xml version="1.0" encoding="UTF-8"?>
<markers>
  <marker title="the redwalls" venue="Knitting Factory" ↦
  lat="40.7173" lng="-74.0053"/>
  <marker title="dirty projectors" venue="Bowery Ballroom" ↦
 lat="40.7205" lng="-73.9937"/>
</markers>
```

RSS: A Timely Format

RDF Site Summary or Really Simple Syndication (RSS)—take your pick—is used throughout the Web to syndicate web content such as blogs and news feeds. RSS, which is a flavor of XML, is typically referred to as a *feed* or *data feed*.

RSS typically stores summaries of blog or news content with links to the content, but RSS is also widely used to syndicate other types of content ranging from event data such as Tourfilter and Upcoming.org to social status updates such as Twitter and Facebook's Status Updates.

Note   You can find more information about RSS and the RSS 2.0 specification at **http://cyber.law.harvard.edu/rss/rss.html**.

For an example of RSS used to syndicate event data, let's take a look at Tourfilter's RSS feed of concert data in New York, shown here. Notice the header information such as title, link, and description. Then the RSS contains a "feed" of "items" that may contain a title, a publication date (**<pubDate>**), and a link. This RSS feed doesn't contain any specific location information such as latitude and longitude, which would make it a GeoRSS feed. (For more information about GeoRSS, check out **http://www.georss.org**.)

```
<?xml version="1.0" encoding="UTF-8"?>
<rss version="2.0">
  <channel>
    <title>tourfilter new york shows</title>
    <link>http://www.tourfilter.com/newyork</link>
    <description>Get an email when bands you like come to New York: ↪
 A community calendar of upcoming local live music.</description>
    <language>en</language>

    <item>
      <title>hot rod circuit (Knitting Factory 12/9)</title>
      <pubDate>Fri, 12 Oct 2007 04:49:09 -0400</pubDate>
      <link>http://www.tourfilter.com/newyork/hot_rod_circuit</link>
    </item>

    <item>
      <title>Michelle Shocked (Highline Ballroom 12/9)</title>
      <pubDate>Mon, 01 Oct 2007 04:50:43 -0400</pubDate>
      <link>http://www.tourfilter.com/newyork/michelle_shocked</link>
</item>
Ib
```

```
</channel>
</rss>
```

JSON: The Programmer-Friendly Format

So, what is this JavaScript Object Notation (JSON) that we all keep hearing about? JSON is your friend, so it's time to learn it and love it. JSON is not necessarily a data feed format but is really a data interchange format. It is basically a simple text format that is a chunk of valid JavaScript that lets you represent data as JavaScript objects. JSON is easy to read and write, which makes it easy to program and debug (by you). And, it's a subset of the JavaScript language, so it's easy to parse data represented as JSON within your JavaScript code.

You can use JSON to store arrays, as well as key/values pairs (typically referred to as a *hash table*, *dictionary*, or *associative array*), which are universal data structures. So, this is a format that can be used across many programming languages and environments.

JSON is becoming widely adopted, especially with the rise of Ajax applications that consume web services, because it is easy to use within these JavaScript-based applications. More and more companies that offer web services, such as Google and Yahoo, are offering JSON output as an alternative to XML.

Let's now see what JSON looks like and how you can use it within JavaScript. Using some of the data from the previous CSV and XML examples, here is the same map marker data in JSON:

```
{
"markers": [
    {
        "title": "the redwalls",
        "venue": "Knitting Factory",
        "lat": 40.7173,
        "lng": -74.0053
    },
```

```
{
    "title": "dirty projectors",
    "venue": "Bowery Ballroom",
    "lat": 40.7205,
    "lng": -73.9937
  }
 ]
}
```

In this example, you are storing the array of **Markers**, denoted by brackets: [ ]. Each marker has a few attributes (**title**, **venue**, **latitude**, and **longitude**) that are stored as key/values pairs (for example, **"title": 'the redwalls'**). Pretty readable, right?

Tip   json.org is great resource for all things JSON. The site provides a good introduction of JSON as well as links to many JSON libraries for a variety of languages. You can also find some examples of JSON formatting and data structures at **http://json.org/example.html**.

Retrieving Remote Content with Mapplet APIs

Google provides three APIs for retrieving remote content for Mapplets. These APIs are part of the Gadget API suite and can be used in both Mapplets and Gadgets. Using the APIs, you can retrieve remote data as text, XML, or JSON. The three API calls are as follows:

- **_IG_FetchContent()** takes a URL as an argument and returns the text from the given URL. This API should be used when working with text or HTML content.

- **_IG_FetchXmlContent()** takes a URL as an argument and returns the XML content as a DOM object. This should be used when retrieving XML content.

- **_IG_FetchFeedAsJSON()** should be used when retrieving RSS or Atom feeds. This takes a URL as an argument and returns the feed as a JSON object.

Note   I won't be covering the `_IG_FetchFeedAsJSON()` API in this chapter. It is a useful API when dealing with RSS and Atom feeds, but this API currently doesn't allow you to parse geographic fields, such as latitude and longitude, from RSS or Atom feeds.

You can find more information about these APIs and fetching remote content within Mapplets and Gadgets at `http://code.google.com/apis/gadgets/docs/remote-content.html`.

Retrieving Text

Let's return to some code examples! You'll start by using the first of Google's "fetch" APIs to retrieve some text from a remote server and display it in the Mapplet. *Text* in this case can refer to any type of text: HTML, CSV data, or even plain, unformatted text. The API `_IG_FetchContent()` will retrieve the remote URL you specify and return the data from the URL as plain text. It's up to your application to use the retrieved text data as needed. If you retrieve HTML, you may want to display the chunk of HTML you've retrieved in your application's user interface. If you retrieve something like CSV-formatted data, you will probably be parsing the data and using some of this data in various parts of your application, such as creating markers on a map.

In the first example, you will fetch some HTML content and display the HTML in a JavaScript `alert()` window. It's a simple example but will show you how the first of Google's "fetch" APIs work.

1.   In the Mapplet Scratch Pad at `http://maps.google.com/maps/mm`, click the "Go back to editor" button to display the scratch pad editor.

2.   Cut and paste the Mapplet XML from `example_2_1_fetch_text.xml`, and paste it into the Mapplet Scratch Pad.

3.   Click the Preview button in the scratch pad. You should see the Mapplet shown in Figure 2-1.

Figure 2-1. HTML from Apress.com displayed in an alert window

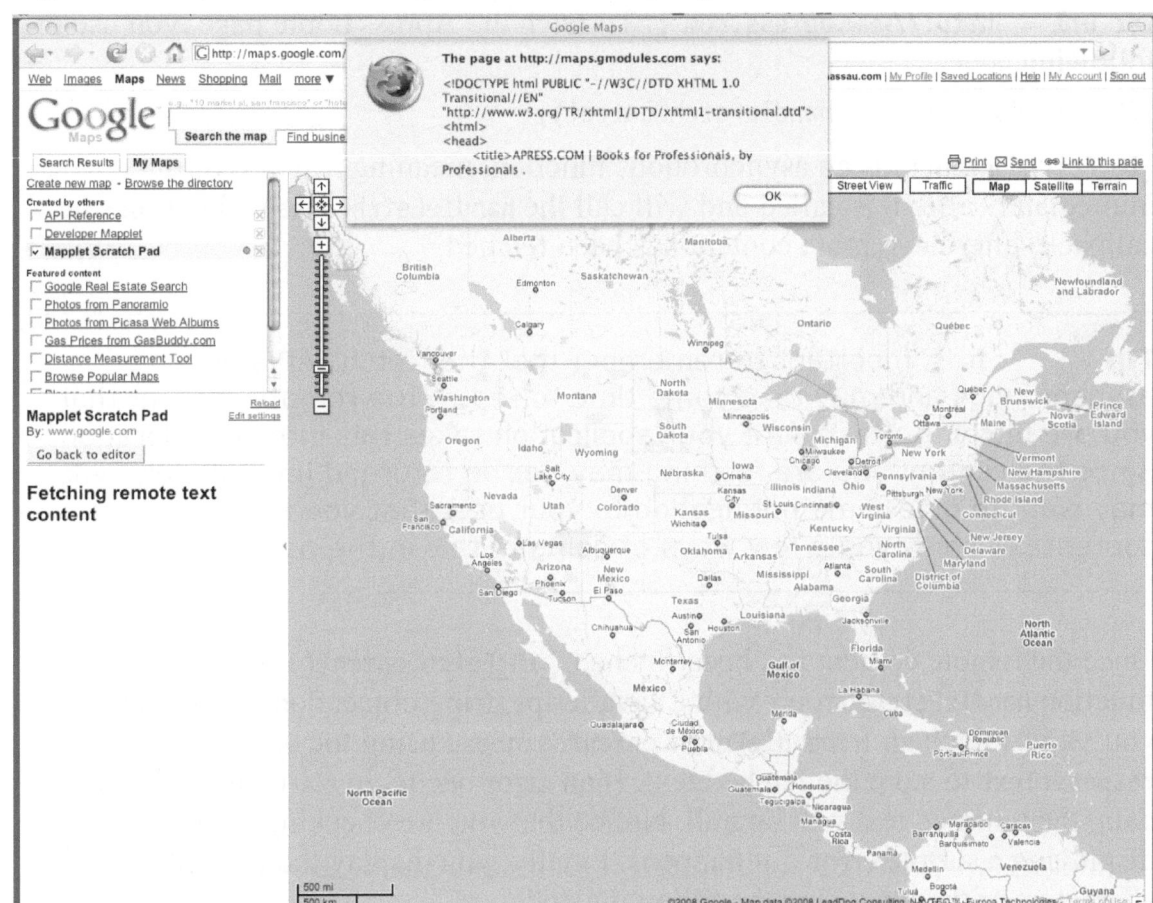

Examining the Code

Congratulations—your Mapplet has successfully fetched some remote content! In this example, you used the **_IG_FetchContent()** API to retrieve the HTML from **www.apress.com**. **_IG_FetchContent()** takes two arguments: the URL that you want to fetch and a function that gets called once the content from the URL has been fetched. Remember, this is referred to as a *callback*. Let's look at this example line by line.

You first create a variable called **url** that contains the Apress home page URL: **var url = "http://www.apress.com";**. To fetch the Apress home page, you use the following code:

_IG_FetchContent(url, handleFetchContent);

_IG_FetchContent() is an asynchronous function, meaning it will return immediately after it is called and will call the **handleFetchContent** function (the callback) after the remote content has been fetched.

Tip   It is important to remember that the "fetch" APIs are asynchronous and may take some time to return the remote content that you are fetching. Make sure your application takes this into consideration. Since the content you are fetching may not be returned immediately, you may want to give some notification to your user that you are retrieving content. I'll show you a few ways of doing of this in the next few examples.

Once the remote content has been fetched, **_IG_FetchContent()** will call the function **handleFetchContent** with a JavaScript string object containing the text you've just fetched. In **handleFetchContent**, you are using the variable **responseText** to store the fetched text. If an error occurs in retrieving the remote data, the returned text will be null. Notice that you are checking for this and displaying a simple error if it happens. Finally, you display the first 200 characters of the text using the following code:
alert(responseText.substr(0,200));.

```
function handleFetchContent (responseText) {
    // check to see if there was an error in the fetch
    if (responseText == null) {
        // an error occurred
        alert("failed to retrieve data from " + url);
        return;
    }
```

```
    // display the text that was returned from apress.com
    // but only display the first 200 characters
    alert(responseText.substr(0,200));
}
```

In the end, you've fetched and displayed the first 200 HTML characters of Apress.com.

Making Mapplets More Interactive

Let's expand on the previous example by retrieving some map-related data; at the same time, you'll make the application more interactive. The previous example didn't give the user any indication you were loading data in the background. You may not have noticed any delay in retrieving and displaying the data, but it's always important to take this possibility into consideration and give your user some indication that the initial data is loading.

With this next example, I'll introduce a few new concepts. First, let's create a link in the application that allows the user to load the remote data with a single click of a link. Second, you will create a status indication in the application to let users know what's going on behind the scenes: whether the data is loading, whether an error has occurred, or whether the data was loaded successfully. Last, let's take the remote data you are fetching and actually display it in your application. You aren't going to add anything to the map itself quite yet—that's coming in one of the next examples.

You haven't focused much on the application portion of the Mapplet yet—the small web page that is displayed in the bottom-left portion of the screen when you are viewing the Mapplet. All you have done so far is use **<h2>** tags to display the title of the sample applications. Let's expand on this in the following example, adding a simple link to load the remote data:

```
<a href="#" onclick="loadData();">Load Data</a>
```

You will also add two HTML tags to the application to display status messages as well as content that you retrieve from the server. These will look like this:

```
<p>status: <span id="status">Nothing loaded yet.</span></p>

<p id="content"></p>
```

Notice the IDs that you've assigned to both the status tag and the content tag. You'll use these IDs to dynamically update the HTML contained within both the status and content tags. I'll explain this after you take a look at the code.

You are also adding some simple CSS to help style the web page portion of the Mapplet. You'll see how easy it is to style your application; in the following example, you are modifying only the font.

In this next example, you will be retrieving data from your own server. As you move forward in this book, a lot of the sample code will need to run from a web server that can be accessible on the Net—not your local machine. In this next example, you'll create a simple CSV data file to store some band and venue information, and the Mapplet will fetch this data from the server. If you don't have access to your own server, you can upload the test files to Google Pages (`http://pages.google.com`) for the next few examples, but you'll need to get access to a server with PHP for some of the upcoming examples in the next chapters.

1. Place the file markers.csv on a public web server that is publicly available. If you don't have access to a public web server, you can upload the markers.csv file to your account at http://pages.google.com. The data in markers.csv looks like this:

   ```
   the redwalls, Knitting Factory, 40.7173, -74.0053, ↪
   dirty projectors, Bowery Ballroom, 40.7205, -73.9937
   ```

2. In the Mapplet Scratch Pad, click the "Go back to editor" button to display the scratch pad editor.

3. Edit the Mapplet source in **example_2_2_fetch_csv.xml**, and make sure the URL in the following line points to your **markers.csv** file:

   ```
   var url = "http://yourserver.com/path/to/markers.csv";
   ```

4. After editing **example_2_2_fetch_csv.xml**, copy and paste the contents of the file into the Mapplet Scratch Pad.

Figure 2-2. Remote content displayed in a Mapplet

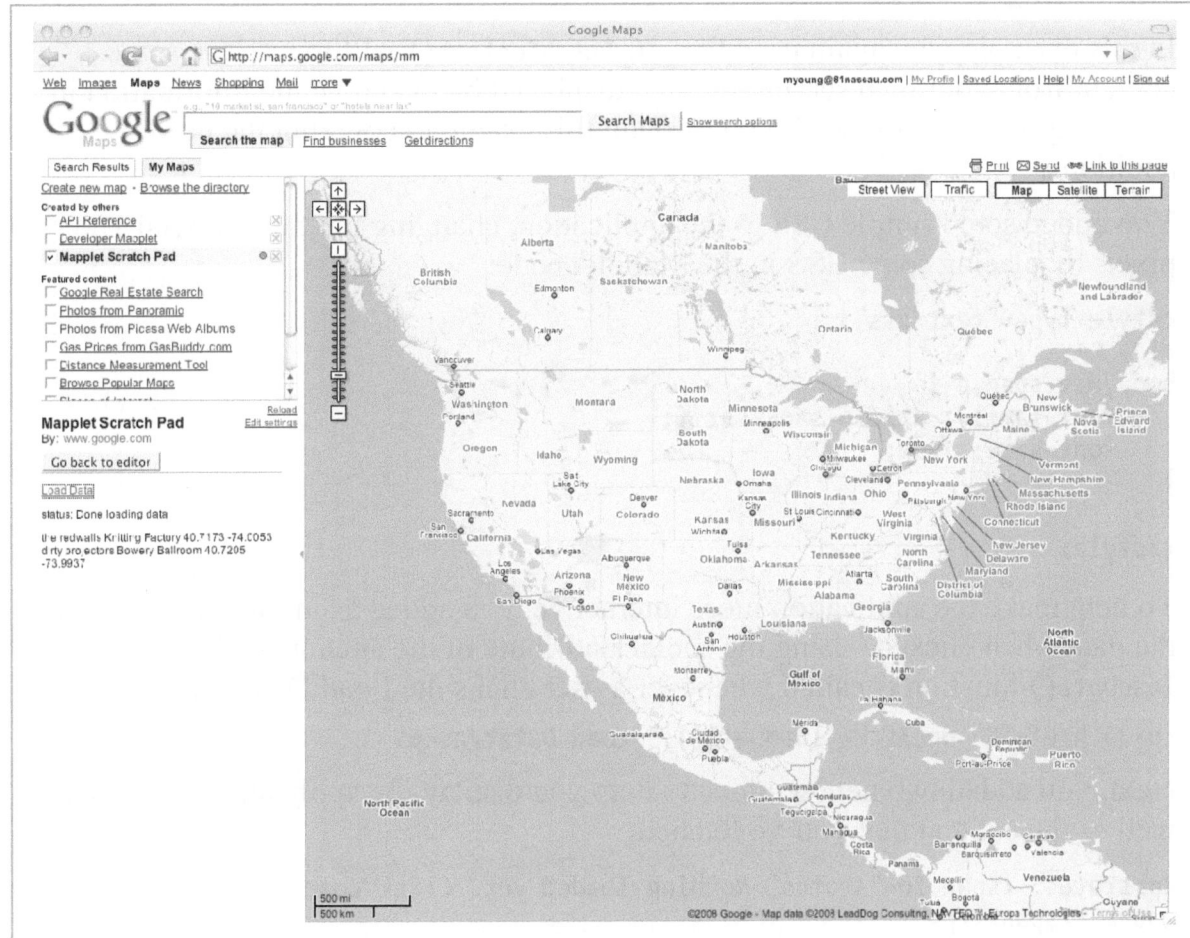

5.   Click the Preview button in the scratch pad. You should see the Mapplet shown in Figure 2-2.

6.   Once the Mapplet loads, click the Load Data link to load the remote marker data.

Examining the Code

In this example, you again used the **_IG_FetchContent()** API to retrieve some content from your own server and then displayed band and venue information in your Mapplet. I'll now walk you through this example, covering the new additions.

You added some simple CSS to the application, changing the font to Arial 12 pixels by placing some CSS in the Mapplet code:

```
<style type="text/css">
<!--
body,div,span,p {
    font-family: arial, sans-serif;
    font-size: 12px;
}
-->
</style>
```

To help make the application more interactive, you added a simple link that loads the data when clicked. Using the **onclick** attribute of the anchor tag, the **loadData()** function is called whenever a user clicks the Load Data link:

```
<p><a href="#" onclick="loadData();">Load Data</a><p>
```

Next, you added two new sections to help you display the application's status as well as the content that you've fetched:

```
<p>status: <span id="status">Nothing loaded yet. Click Load Data
above.</span></p>

<p id="content"></p>
```

To update the status and content, you're using the function **_gel()** to get access to the DOM element that you need to update (**status** and **content** in this case). **_gel()** is Google's wrapper for the JavaScript function **getElementById()**, which gives you the DOM element for the specified ID. So, to update the HTML between the **<span id="status">** and **</span>** tags, you use the following:

```
_gel("status").innerHTML = "loading...";
```

Notice that you update the status with "loading" when you first call `loadData()` and then update it again if either an error occurs when fetching the data or you successfully fetch the remote data.

After you successfully fetch the band and venue data, you parse the data (which is one long string of comma-delimited fields) into an array using the JavaScript `split()` function. Once you have the data in the array `markerData`, you loop over the array, adding each field to the `displayHTML` variable. Notice that you need to add a line break (`<br/>`) after every fourth field is pulled from the array; you do this since the marker data holds four fields for every marker: band name, venue name, latitude, and longitude.

```
// use the split to parse the incoming marker data
var markerData = responseText.split(",");

// loop over the individual marker data fields
for (var i = 0; i < markerData.length; i++) {
    //...
}
```

You finally update the application's content section with the following command:

```
_gel("content").innerHTML = displayHTML;
```

Retrieving XML

Chances are good that most of the third-party data that you'll be dealing with when creating mashups will be some flavor of XML. Fortunately, using Google's `_IG_FetchXmlContent()` API as well as built-in JavaScript functions to parse the XML, it's fairly easy to use XML content in Mapplets. Over the next few examples, you'll see how to create a Mapplet that fetches remote XML data.

This next example is similar to the previous example. You will be retrieving the same data as XML instead of CSV. You'll see how to use the Google API to fetch XML content as well as learn how to parse XML within your Mapplet. This example won't touch the map, but you will get there in the next example—I promise! I know you've been waiting.

1. Place the file markers.xml on a public web server. Again, if you don't have access to a public web server, you can upload the file to your account at http://pages.google.com. The data in markers.xml looks like the following:

```xml
<?xml version="1.0" encoding="UTF-8"?>
<markers>
    <marker title="the redwalls" venue="Knitting Factory" ⮑
  lat="40.7173" lng="-74.0053" />
    <marker title="dirty projectors" venue="Bowery Ballroom" ⮑
  lat="40.7205" lng="-73.9937" />
</markers>
```

2. In the Mapplet Scratch Pad, click the "Go back to editor" button to display the scratch pad editor.

3. Edit the Mapplet source in example_2_3_fetch_xml.xml, and make sure the URL in the following line points to your markers.xml file:

```
var url = "http://yourserver.com/path/to/markers.xml";
```

4. After editing example_2_3_fetch_xml.xml, copy and paste the contents of the file into the Mapplet Scratch Pad.

5. Click the Preview button in the scratch pad. You should see the Mapplet shown in Figure 2-3.

6. Once the Mapplet loads, click the Load Data link to load the remote marker data.

Figure 2-3. XML data displayed in a Mapplet

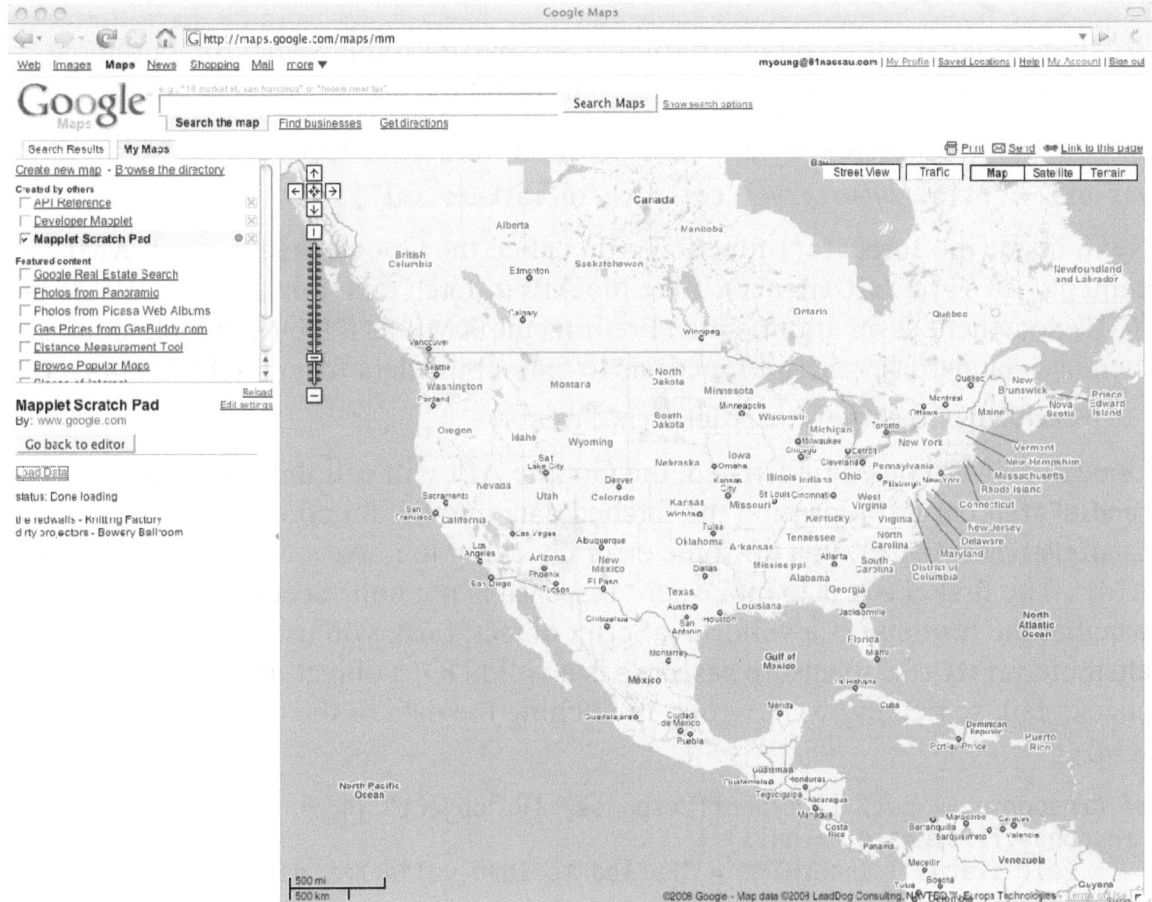

Examining the Code

So, there you have it—you just retrieved and parsed some XML from a remote server! Let's take a quick look at what's new in this one.

First, you should have changed the **url** to point to your own **markers.xml** file:

```
var url = "http://yourserver.com/path/to/markers.xml";
```

Next, inside the **loadData()** function, you called the Google API to fetch XML content: **_IG_FetchXmlContent()**. Like the API to fetch text, this takes a URL to an XML document as an argument and returns the XML as a DOM object. You can then use standard JavaScript functions to extract the data from the DOM object.

```
_IG_FetchXmlContent(url, handleFetchContent);
```

Once the XML content is fetched, the Google API will call the function **handleFetchContent()**, passing the fetched data into the function. At the top of **handleFetchContent()**, you do some error checking to make sure the data is valid XML. The first check is to make sure **response** is not null. Second, you check whether the response is a valid JavaScript object. Last, you use the DOM attribute **firstChild** to ensure **response** is a valid DOM object. If any of those checks fail, something went wrong in fetching the data or the data isn't valid XML.

```
if (response == null || typeof(response) != "object" || ↵
 response.firstChild == null) {
    _gel("status").innerHTML = "Failed to load valid XML data";
    return;
}
```

If you have valid XML to work with, the previous validation checks will all pass with flying colors. Next, you use the **getElementsByTagName()** DOM function to get each of the markers from the XML. **getElementsByTagName()** will search the DOM object and return an array of DOM elements matching the name you are looking for (**marker** in this case). You use the following line to get each of the marker elements:

```
var markers = response.getElementsByTagName("marker");
```

The variable markers now contains an array of DOM elements. Next, it's a matter of looping over the markers array, extracting all the information for each marker—band/title, venue name, latitude, and longitude. Since all this information was stored as attributes in the marker XML elements (<marker title="the redwalls" venue="Knitting Factory" lat="40.7173" lng="-74.0053" />), you can use the DOM function getAttribute() to extract each of the fields from the marker element. After you extract each of the fields, you add the title and venue to the displayHTML variable, which is then rendered to the screen of the application.

```
for (var i = 0; i < markers.length; i++) {
    var marker  = markers[i];

    var title = marker.getAttribute("title");
    var venue = marker.getAttribute("venue");
    var lat = marker.getAttribute("lat");
    var lng = marker.getAttribute("lng");

    displayHTML += "<div>" + title + " - " + venue + "</div>";
}
```

Notice that you didn't do anything with the latitude and longitude? That's coming in the next example, when you combine everything you've learned from this chapter with some of the Mapplet APIs from the previous chapter. Are you ready? Good, let's move on.

Mapping Remote XML Data

At this point, you have a lot of tools that you can pull together into a single application. You now know how to retrieve XML content from a remote server, as well as plot data on a map using the Mapplet APIs. Let's use all your new skills to plot some remote data on a map! It's about time, right? You'll even add a little interactivity so that your map responds to clicks from your user.

You'll use some of the code from the previous example, retrieving the same marker XML data from your own server. But, instead of just displaying the list of band and venues in the left panel of your Mapplet, let's actually map the venues on the map. You'll also use code from the previous chapter to help you create the markers on the map and center the map so that you can view all the markers on the map at the same time.

Before you get started with the code, let's first take a look at the Mapplet you are going to create. Notice in Figure 2-4 that you have a list of the bands and venues on the left side and markers placed on the maps for the venue locations? You're adding some new interactivity to this application. When you click one of the band/venue links on the left, the info window for that corresponding marker will open on the map. It's always a good idea to let your user navigate the content through either the list or the map.

Figure 2-4. XML data displayed on the map

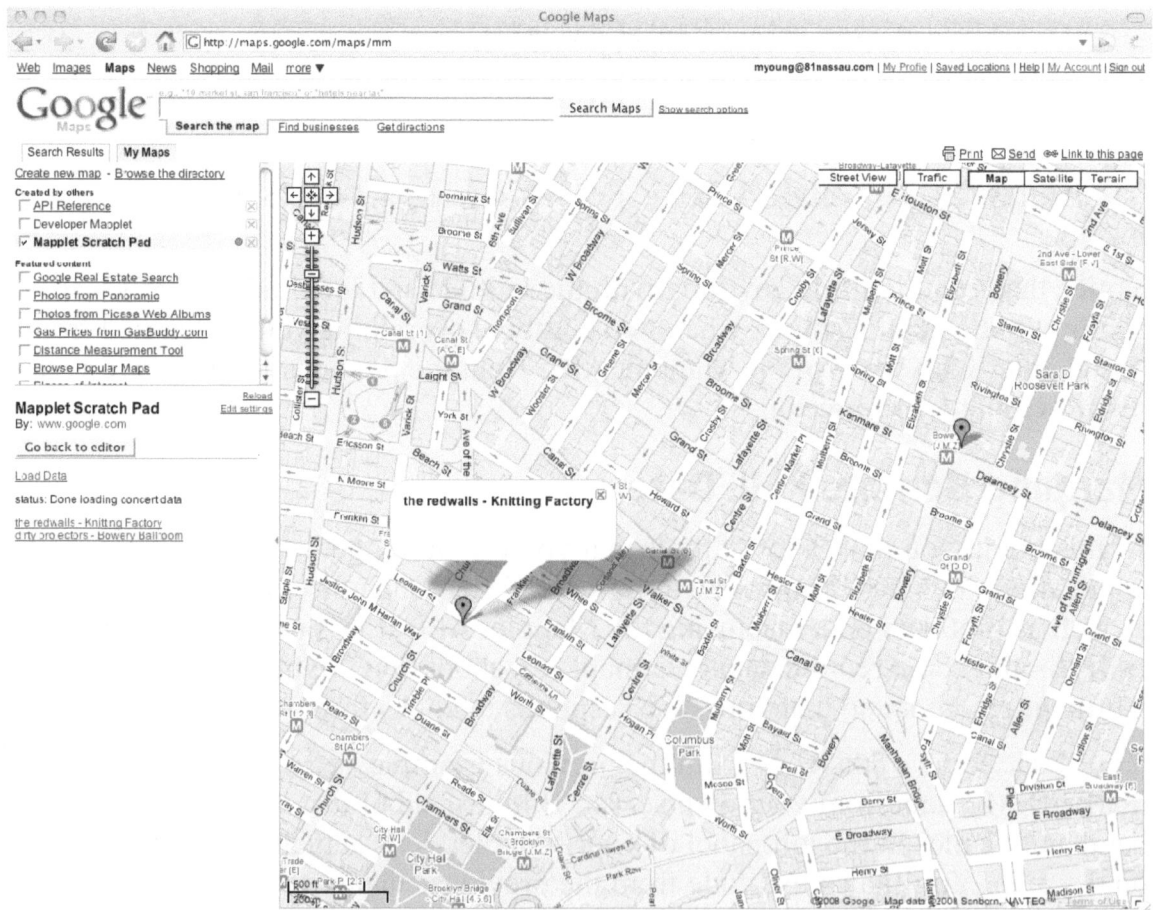

Follow these steps to view the latest Mapplet:

1. You'll be using the same markers.xml file you set up in the previous example.

2. In the Mapplet Scratch Pad, click the "Go back to editor" button to display the scratch pad editor.

3. Edit the Mapplet source in example_2_4_plot_remote_data.xml, and make sure the URL in the following line points to your markers.xml file:

    ```
    var url = "http://yourserver.com/path/to/markers.xml";
    ```

4. After editing example_2_4_plot_remote_data.xml, copy and paste the contents of the file into the Mapplet Scratch Pad.

5. Click the Preview button in the scratch pad. You should see the Mapplet shown in Figure 2-4.

6. Once the Mapplet loads, click the Load Data link to load the remote marker data. Once the band and venue data is loaded, you should see markers on the map as well as a list of band and venue links on the left side of your application. Click the band/venue links on the left, and notice how the appropriate info window appears.

Examining the Code

You have seen most of the code in this example, but a few new things are happening. Let's take a look at these now.

After you successfully load the data, you first check to make sure you have at least one marker in your XML file. If not, you show an error message:

```
if (concertData.length == 0) {
    _gel("status").innerHTML = "Sorry, we don't have any concert data at this
time";
    return;
}
```

Once you know you have at least one marker in your XML data, you need to properly initialize a few map-related variables before you start placing markers on the map and updating your application. First, you create a new **GLatLngBounds** object **bounds**. Remember from the previous chapter that the **bounds** object is used to center the map based on all the points you plot on the map. Second, you call a function that you've created called **cleanupMarkers()**. This function removes event listeners added to the map markers. (You add event listeners to notify you when an event occurs, such as when a marker is clicked. You haven't added any markers to the map yet in the code, but it's coming next.) It's important to remove the event listeners in case the users click the Load Data button multiple times—you need to get in the habit of clearing up any markers and event listeners that you aren't using before you load new ones.

```
var bounds = new GLatLngBounds();

cleanupMarkers();

// function to remove all marker Event Listeners
function cleanupMarkers() {
        if (markers == null)
                return;

        for (var i = 0; i < markers.length; i++) {
                var marker = markers[i];
                GEvent.clearListeners(marker, "click");
        }
}
```

Tip   It's important to remove any event listeners that you aren't using anymore. This comes into account when you reload data or load new data sets from an application and are removing event listeners that aren't being used anymore. You can remove event listeners in a few ways, depending on how they were created: **GEvent.removeListenerstner()**, **GEvent.clearListeners()**, or **GEvent.clearInstanceListeners()**. Consult the Mapplet API reference for more details.

Before creating more markers, you reinitialize the array, **markers**, that stores all the **GMarker** objects you'll add to the map. You need to keep track of the markers so that you can display the proper marker info window when a band/venue link is clicked in your application. You'll learn more about this in a moment.

```
markers = new Array();
```

Next, you loop through all the marker data found in the XML file that was just retrieved. The latitude and longitude is parsed from the XML and is used to create a **GLatLng** point. You then call the function **createMarker()** to create a new marker, passing in the band name (title) and venue name, which are used to decorate the marker info window. Once the marker is created, you place it on the map.

```
var point = new GLatLng(lat, lng);
var marker = createMarker(point, title + " - " + venue);
```

```
map.addOverlay(marker);
```

After the marker has been placed on the map, you add it to your array, **markers**. You need a reference to each marker, because you'll need to display the marker's info window if a user happens to click a link in your application that corresponds with the marker.

```
markers[i] = marker;
```

You add a link to the Mapplet's left panel of the application for each concert in the XML data. Notice that the link calls a function called **clickMarker()** with an argument of the marker index. The **clickMarker()** function helps you display the marker's info window when the link is clicked. This is key in making your Mapplet interactive, because the user can now either explore using the map or the list of concert links. Notice that in **clickMarker()** you use the **GEvent.trigger()** function to trigger the "click" action on the maker. This forces the "onclick" event on the marker, which in turn displays the info window for that marker.

```
displayHTML += "<div><a href='#' onclick='clickMarker(" + i + ");'>" + ⮠
 title + " - " + venue + "</a></div>";
```

```
function clickMarker(index) {
    GEvent.trigger(markers[index], "click");
}
```

Finally, once you've created all the markers, you use the getBoundsZoomLevelAsync() function to help you scale the map so that you can see all the markers (two in this case) at the same time. You don't actually update the Mapplet application with your list of concert data until the map is properly centered and scaled.

Google's Data Cache

Google caches all data that is retrieved using the _IG_FetchContent() and _IG_FetchXmlContent() APIs. The data is cached to help speed up the retrieval of the data in your Mapplets and also to reduce load on the remote server (in case your Mapplet gets a lot of users at once). If the content you are fetching is refreshed more than once an hour, you need to use the refreshInterval parameter to bypass the cache and fetch the latest content from the remote server. You can use this parameter, which is measured in seconds, to specify the interval at which you want to refresh the cached data. You'll use this parameter in your applications in the next chapter, but here's what it looks like if you need to refresh your data every 10 minutes:

```
_IG_FetchXMLContent("http://yourserver.com/path/to/markers.xml", ↦
 callback, { refreshInterval: (60 * 10) });
```

Note If you do use the refreshInterval to bypass the cache, Google recommends you use a range of 60 (one minute) to 3600 seconds (one hour).

Summary

Nice job. You've created an interactive map using data from a remote server! I hope you are starting to see the power of combining remote data feeds and services with a map. You're just getting started.

Over the next few chapters, you'll start mapping live data from real web services. You now have the tools to start creating your mashup. Are you ready? Let's move on....

Part 2: Creating the Mashup

Chapter 3: Geocoding Web Content

There is plenty of great content on the Web that's just begging to be mapped! You may even have some content of your own that you'd like to map. This chapter provides numerous examples of how to geocode web content, which is the first step in creating a map-based mashup.

To geocode web content, you have to identify the content to be plotted. Once you have selected the content, you geocode the content so that it can be mapped. Remember that *geocoding* is the process of converting a location, such as an address, into a latitude/longitude pair. That latitude/longitude pair is the "meat" of location-based mashups and is what's needed to actually plot data on a map.

In this chapter, you will learn the basics of a server-side mashup, including the following:

- Identifying good web content for mashups
- Retrieving and parsing Tourfilter's concert RSS feeds
- Parsing location data from Tourfilter's feeds
- Geocoding concert venues using Eventful's APIs

Identifying Good Content for Mashups

So, what content works well in map-based mashups? It's pretty simple—any content that has some association with location. Plenty of feeds and APIs are available that provide content with location-based content that can be used in a mashup: news, photos, real estate listings, and concert and events.

Once you have an idea for a mashup or have a data source you want to map, you must figure out how to extract the location information for the data source. The "trick" in building a map-based mashup is determining the latitude and longitude of your content—remember that the latitude and longitude are needed to place the content on a map. Some data feeds and APIs will provide the latitude and longitude of their content, but most do not. In most cases, it's up to you to convert the location found in the data (city name, address, building name, state, and so on) into a latitude/longitude pair. I faced this same problem when I built my first Google Maps mashup. Let me explain....

When the Google Maps API became public in 2005, I went about building my first Google Maps mashup. I wanted to create a news-based mashup that plotted news feeds on a Google map. Extracting the location from the text of news stories isn't an easy task, but the Associated Press (AP) includes a location in the dateline of each of its stories. Look at the following AP news headline and description, taken from an AP news RSS feed:

Skydiver Completes 640 Jumps in 24 Hours

GREENSBURG, Ind. (AP) -- Jay Stokes celebrated his 50th birthday by jumping out of an airplane—640 times....

Notice the "GREENBURG, Ind" at the beginning of the story? This was a key discovery in creating my news mashup. I then wrote code to parse the story location from the beginning of each story, query a Geocode web service to translate the location to a latitude/longitude pair, and then map each story on a Google map. It was simple in concept and implementation!

Figure 3-1 shows my news mashup, which you can find at
`http://81nassau.com/apnews`.

Figure 3-1. AP + Google Maps mashup: http://81nassau.com/apnews

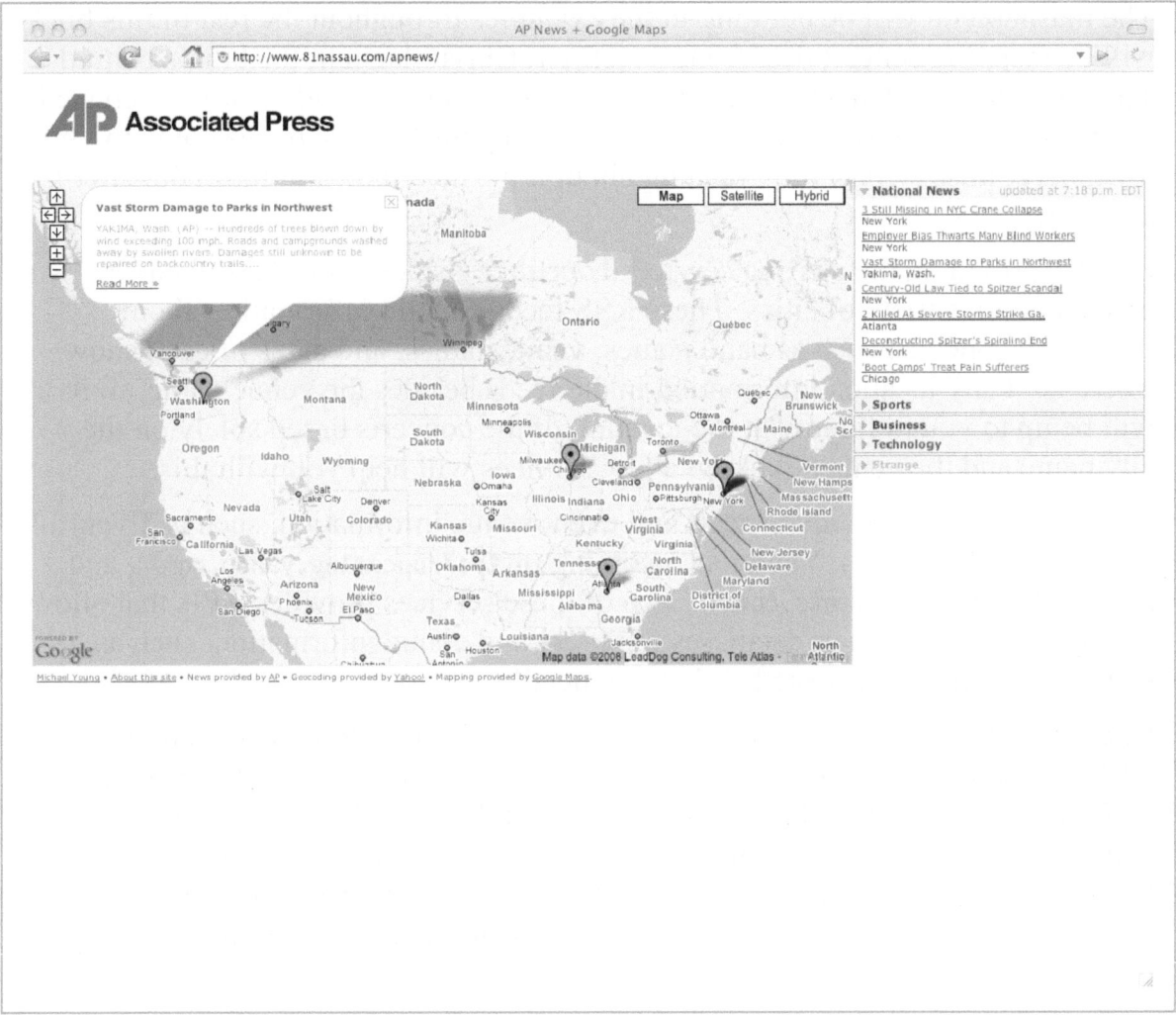

Your Mashup Data Sources: Tourfilter and Eventful

The mashup you will be building in the examples throughout the rest of this book will be mapping concert data from Tourfilter. Chris Marstall, the brains behind Tourfilter, has created a brilliant site—you enter a list of bands you're interested in tracking, and Tourfilter will email you when your favorite bands come to your town. Ever miss a concert by reading about it the next day? Me too. Tourfilter is a savior.

Besides providing the alerting service, Tourfilter also provides RSS feeds of concerts for a variety of cities. These RSS feeds contain information about upcoming concerts, such as band names, venue names, and dates of each show. There isn't any location information in the feeds besides the venue name, so it will be up to you to figure out the location of the concerts based solely on the city name and the venue. Luckily, a few services will help you with this.

Plenty of services provide concert and event venue information, such as Eventful (`http://eventful.com/`), Yahoo's Upcoming (`http://upcoming.yahoo.com/`), and Zvents (`http://www.zvents.com/`). Each of these services provides APIs that allow developers to query their databases for event and venue information, such as venue location. This is exactly what you need!

One interesting note about Upcoming is that besides providing event and listing APIs, it also provides GeoRSS feeds of events for various cities. As mentioned earlier, GeoRSS is an RSS feed with latitude and longitude information contained within the feed. You could use Upcoming's GeoRSS feeds and plot that on a map with Google Mapplets, since it has already geocoded the event and concert data for you. That would be a perfectly good mashup, but it defeats the purpose of learning how to geocode the content yourself.

For the examples in this chapter, you will use Eventful's (formerly known as the Events and Venues Database, or EVDB) APIs to help you search for the location of each venue in Tourfilter's concert RSS feeds.

Note   Map-based mashups typically require the use of a geocode service to help geocode your content's location. A geocode service will convert a location, such as a city or street address, to latitude and longitude. In the case of the Eventful venue search API, it does the heavy lifting for you and provides the address, city, latitude, and longitude for each venue in its database. So, a geocoding service isn't necessary in this chapter's examples.

So, to recap, your mashup is going to need to do the following:

1. Fetch Tourfilter's concert RSS data and extract the band, venue, and concert date.

2. Look up the location (latitude/longitude) of each venue using the Eventful venue search API.

Once you have this down, you'll learn how to map the Tourfilter data in a Google Mapplet in the following chapters. Sounds simple, right? It is—you'll see.

The Boring (But Important) Requirements

Before you jump in to the code, you need to ensure you have the proper software installed on your server. You also need to set up a developer account on Eventful's developer site so you can use its API. Please make sure you have all the following installed before continuing:

Web server with PHP 5: The following samples require an Internet-connected web server with PHP 5. If you are still using PHP 4 (oh, you're the one...I heard about you), no fear. Please read on to see what you'll need.

SimpleXML: You will be using the SimpleXML library to parse XML documents in the following examples. SimpleXML comes standard with PHP 5. As the name implies, SimpleXML makes it easy to parse XML files. If you are new to SimpleXML, I suggest reading up on it briefly at `http://www.php.net/simplexml`. If you don't have PHP 5 on your server, you can use the XML library MiniXML at `http://minixml.sourceforge.net`. MiniXML doesn't require any external libraries and will be easy to install and use regardless of your hosting setup. However, you will need to modify the following code samples to use the MiniXML library instead of SimpleXML.

CURL: CURL is a tool used to communicate with remote servers via HTTP, HTTPS, FTP, and many other protocols. For the examples in this book, we'll be using CURL to make simple HTTP requests to retrieve data from your data sources: Tourfilter and Eventful. CURL does not come with PHP by default, but most web hosts have CURL enabled, so you should be fine. If you do need to install CURL on your server, this is a good place to start: `http://us.php.net/curl`.

Determining Whether You Have the Proper Software Installed

If you aren't entirely sure whether you have PHP 5, SimpleXML, and CURL installed, you can create a simple PHP script to display all sorts of information about your PHP setup. Create a PHP script using the code in Listing 3-1, upload to your web server, and view it in a browser. Take a look at the output to confirm your version of PHP and that you have SimpleXML and CURL installed.

Listing 3-1. Output the Current State of PHP on Your Server

```php
<?php

phpinfo();

?>
```

Getting an Eventful Developer Account

There is one last step before you move on. Before you can use the Eventful APIs, you need to sign up for a developer account and obtain an application key. You can do this at Eventful's developer site (`http://api.evdb.com`). To obtain the application key, you will need to provide a little information about yourself and the application you are building, as well as agreeing to Eventful's terms of service. By agreeing to terms of service, you agree to use its data in a noncommercial web application only.

Using Third-Party Content in Your Own Applications

When using third-party content or APIs in your applications, it is important that you comply with the content or API provider's terms of service. There are many legal and copyright issues around using third-party content, so it is important to get written permission from the provider before you use their content or API in your application. If you are unable to get permission, consult a lawyer on the legal and copyright issues.

Chris Marstall, from Tourfilter, has been kind enough to let us use his RSS feeds for the purpose of this book. I'll let you thank Chris on your own. If you go beyond anything specified in this book when using Tourfilter's data, make sure you link to the Tourfilter site using the URLs from Tourfilter's feeds.

Retrieving Tourfilter Concert RSS Feeds

It's time to start writing some code!

Let's start developing the mashup by first retrieving some content—in this case, it will be Tourfilter's concert feed. Tourfilter currently provides an RSS feed of concert data for about 60 cities. You'll end up using each city feed eventually, but for the following samples you'll use New York. The RSS feed for concerts in New York, ordered by concert date, is at
`http://www.tourfilter.com/newyork/rss/by_concert_date`.

Listing 3-2 shows a truncated sample of the New York concert RSS feed. Notice the format of each `<title>` tag, which contains the band name, venue name, and concert date. We'll explore this more in the next example, because we'll need to parse that field to get each of those fields individually. Remember that you're after the venue name, because it and the city name are the only pieces of location-specific information in this data feed!

Listing 3-2. Sample of New York Concert RSS from Tourfilter (Truncated)

```
<?xml version="1.0" encoding="UTF-8"?>
<rss version="2.0">
  <channel>
    <title>tourfilter new york shows</title>
    <link>http://www.tourfilter.com/newyork</link>
    <description>Get an email when bands you like come to New York: ↪
 A community calendar of upcoming local live music.</description>
    <language>en</language>

    <item>
      <title>the double stops (Bitter End 12/31)</title>
      <pubDate>Thu, 20 Dec 2007 05:05:01 -0400</pubDate>
      <link>http://www.tourfilter.com/newyork/the_double_stops</link>
      <guid>50434</guid>
    </item>

    <item>
      <title>new deal (Highline Ballroom 12/31)</title>
      <pubDate>Mon, 01 Oct 2007 04:50:54 -0400</pubDate>
      <link>http://www.tourfilter.com/newyork/new_deal</link>
      <guid>42414</guid>
    </item>

</channel>
</rss>
```

In the first code example in Listing 3-3, you'll use CURL to retrieve the RSS feed from Tourfilter and then use SimpleXML to parse each item from the feed. For now, you'll just print each item field to the screen: title, pubDate, link, and guid. The code in Listing 3-3, from example_3_1_retrieve_tourfilter.php, shows how this is done.

Listing 3-3. Retrieve and Parse Tourfilter's New York Concert Feed

```php
<?php

# Parse Tourfilter's RSS Feed of New York Concerts
# Requires SimpleXML (php5) and curl

header("Content-type: text/plain");

$url = "http://www.tourfilter.com/newyork/rss/by_concert_date";

// set up curl
$ch = curl_init();
curl_setopt($ch, CURLOPT_HEADER, false);
curl_setopt($ch, CURLOPT_RETURNTRANSFER, true);
curl_setopt($ch, CURLOPT_USERAGENT, ➡
'My Curl API Client (http://mysite.com) ' . phpversion());
curl_setopt($ch, CURLOPT_URL, $url);

// make the http request and close up curl
$response = curl_exec($ch);
curl_close($ch);

// make sure we get a response
if (!$response) {
    die("Error: we didn't get any data from $url\n");
}

// parse the response - no error checking for now
$sxml = simplexml_load_string($response);

// loop through each <item> found in the RSS feed
foreach ($sxml->channel->item as $item) {
    print "title: " . $item->title . "\n";
    print "pub date: " . $item->pubDate . "\n";
    print "link: " . $item->link . "\n";
    print "guid: " . $item->guid . "\n\n";
}

?>
```

Running the script **example_3_1_retrieve_tourfilter.php** produces output in Listing 3-4.

Listing 3-4. Sample Output from Your Script (Truncated)

```
title: the double stops (Bitter End 12/31)
pub date: Thu, 20 Dec 2007 05:05:01 -0400
link: http://www.tourfilter.com/newyork/the_double_stops
guid: 50434

title: new deal (Highline Ballroom 12/31)
pub date: Mon, 01 Oct 2007 04:50:54 -0400
link: http://www.tourfilter.com/newyork/new_deal
guid: 42414

title: les savy fav (Bowery Ballroom 12/31)
pub date: Sat, 24 Nov 2007 04:47:56 -0400
link: http://www.tourfilter.com/newyork/les_savy_fav
guid: 47636

title: Circa Survive (Starland Ballroom 12/31)
pub date: Fri, 14 Dec 2007 05:02:00 -0400
link: http://www.tourfilter.com/newyork/circa_survive
guid: 49896
```

Examining the Code

You just retrieved and parsed an RSS feed—nice! Let's walk through the code, since this was your first look at CURL and SimpleXML. If you don't have CURL or SimpleXML installed properly, PHP will let you know, outputting error messages instead of the nice output in Listing 3-4.

First, you set the output of the script to **text/plain** using **header("Content-type: text/plain");**. This makes it easier to read your **print** statements if you are viewing the output on a web page. Without it, you'd need to use **
** tags instead of newlines (**"\n"**), because PHP's output defaults to **text/html**.

Next, you retrieve the RSS feed using PHP's CURL functions. **curl_init()** initializes CURL for you and returns a handle to your CURL object that you use in the rest of the script. **curl_setopt()** is then used to set the CURL parameters that you need. You don't need CURL to return the HTTP header of your HTTP request, so you set **CURLOPT_HEADER** to false. Then, you set **CURLOPT_RETURNTRANSFER** to true, which tells CURL to return the remote data you are fetching to a variable in your script.

The option **CURLOPT_USERAGENT** is used to set the **User-Agent** string in your HTTP request. The **User-Agent** string is one of the HTTP headers and is used to identify you (meaning your HTTP client software). The **User-Agent** string is used in all web browsers, web spiders, and other HTTP clients. You should modify this line to include your name, e-mail, or URL—this is done so that any site you access using this code can get in touch with you if you happen to hit their site too often and exceed their rate limits. You are using good etiquette by doing this.

```
curl_setopt($ch, CURLOPT_USERAGENT, ➥
 'My Curl API Client (http://mysite.com) ' . phpversion());
```

Next, you tell CURL the URL of the RSS feed to retrieve using **curl_setopt($ch, CURLOPT_URL, $url)**. To make the actual HTTP request, you call **curl_exec()**, passing in the CURL handle **$ch**. The response from the server is returned and stored in the variable **$response**:

```
$response = curl_exec($ch);
```

After closing up your CURL connection and doing a little error checking to ensure you got a valid response from Tourfilter, you use SimpleXML to parse the RSS feed. **simplexml_load_string($response)** parses the response into a **SimpleXMLElement** object, which is used to loop over all the **item** tags contained in the RSS feed:

```
// loop through each <item> found in the RSS feed
foreach ($sxml->channel->item as $item) {
    print "title: "    . $item->title . "\n";
    print "pub date: " . $item->pubDate . "\n";
    print "link: "     . $item->link . "\n";
    print "guid: "     . $item->guid . "\n\n";
}
```

Parsing Venue Location from the Tourfilter Feeds

Looking at the **title** field in the Tourfilter RSS feed, you see that it has the following format: `band name (venue name month/date)`. Figure 3-2 illustrates an example of the **title** field format, where the band name is new deal, the venue is Highline Ballroom, and the concert date is 12/31.

Figure 3-2. Current Tourfilter format example

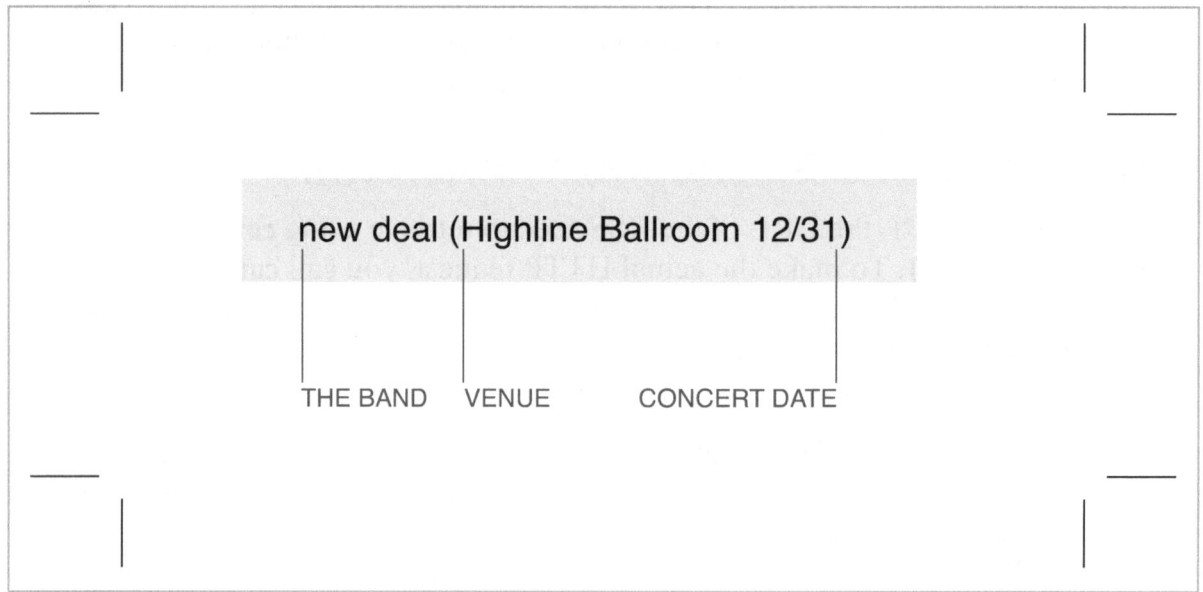

Caution   The format shown in Figure 3-2 is the current format used by Tourfilter, but it could change at any time! When "scraping" data from web sites, it is important to detect and respond to any changes in the data format. If you do not have a written agreement with the content provider, it is not their responsibility to notify you if they change their format. When dealing with data feeds like this, the format will change—trust me on this! We'll look at simple ways of detecting changes in the data format in the following examples.

In the next example, you'll parse each **title** field in the Tourfilter XML to extract the individual band, venue, and concert date fields. You'll use PHP regular expressions to parse these fields. If you've worked with regular expressions before, great! If not, don't fear. Regular expressions are powerful but can also be quite complicated. I won't cover them much here, but I will include enough to get you by. As a refresher, I recommended reading up on PHP's regular expressions support here: **http://www.php.net/pcre**.

The code in **example_3_2_parse_tourfilter.php** contains two regular expression statements that parse the band, venue, and date from the **title** field. This parsing can be done in a single regular expression, but doing it in two makes it slightly easier to read (and to explain!). Run the script **example_3_2_parse_tourfilter.php**, and then I'll dive into the explanation. Running the script will produce output similar to Listing 3-5.

Listing 3-5. Parsing the Band, Venue, and Date (Truncated)

```
title: rebirth brass band (Maxwell's 12/30)
band:  'rebirth brass band'
venue: 'Maxwell's'
date:  '12/30'

title: Talib Kweli (Highline Ballroom 12/30)
band:  'Talib Kweli'
venue: 'Highline Ballroom'
date:  '12/30'

title: bogmen (Nokia Theatre 12/30)
band:  'bogmen'
venue: 'Nokia Theatre'
date:  '12/30'

title: emergency party (Goodbye Blue Monday 12/30)
band:  'emergency party'
venue: 'Goodbye Blue Monday'
date:  '12/30'
```

Examining the Code

The code in **example_3_2_parse_tourfilter.php** starts similarly to the previous example, with fetching the RSS feed and looping through each **item** found in the feed.

Inside the **foreach** loop, the **title**, **band**, **venue**, and **date** variables are initialized. At this point, the **title** data is stored in the **$title** variable. Now it's time to parse the band name, venue name, and date from **$item**, using PHP's **preg_match** function.

preg_match looks for a pattern in a string and parses the string according to the supplied pattern. **preg_match** takes three arguments: the regular expression pattern, the string you want to match the pattern against, and an array that will be populated with any matches that are found in the string.

The first regular expression is used to parse the band name and the venue/date from **$title**. You'll separate the venue name and the date in the next regular expression. If, for example, the string **$title** contains **new deal (Highline Ballroom 12/31)**, you'll parse it into two parts with the first regular expression: the first part being the band name and the second part being everything contained inside the parentheses (the venue name and date). So after running **$title** through the first regular expression, you will have two new variables storing the band and venue/date: **new deal** and **Highline Ballroom 12/31**. Let's take a look at the first regular expression, or *regex*, as it's called:

```
preg_match("/^(.*)[\s]*\((.*)\)$/", $title, $matches);
```

You're probably saying, "Ugh, what the *!@# is that?" (Sorry, that's my poor regular expression humor.) Let's take a look at that first argument in **preg_match**, which is the pattern you are using to parse the string **$title**. Figure 3-3 displays the pattern, showing the parts of the regular expression that match the **band** and **venue/date** fields.

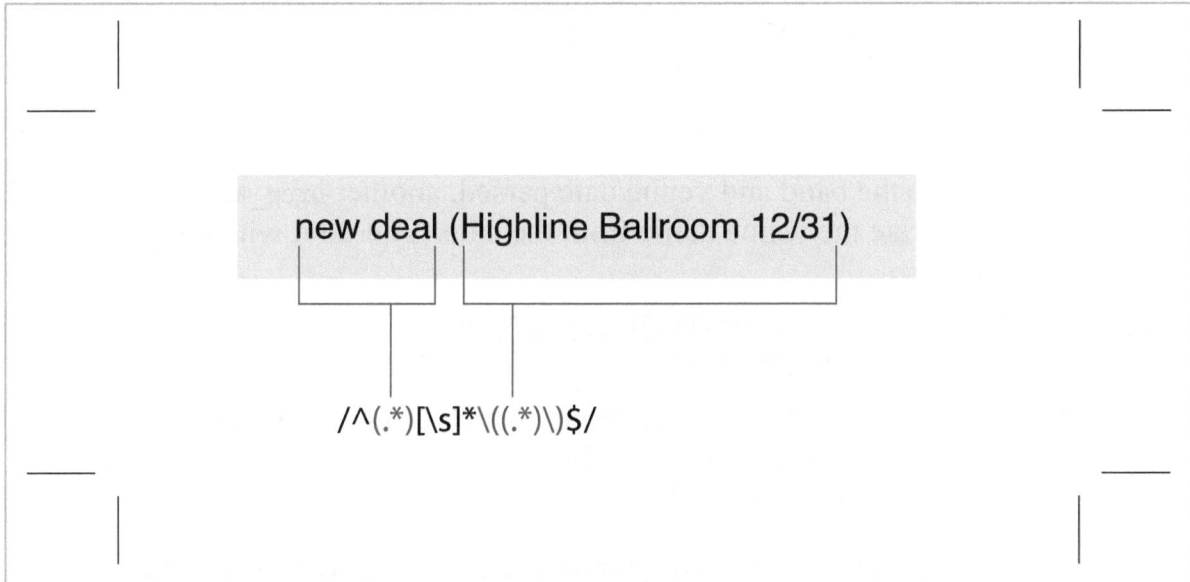

Once you run the string **$title** through the **preg_match**, the **$matches** array will now hold the subpatterns you specified in the regex. If a successful match is made, **$matches** will hold three strings and look like the following:

```
Array
(
    [0] => new deal (Highline Ballroom 12/31)
    [1] => new deal
    [2] => Highline Ballroom 12/31
)
```

After the **preg_match**, a check is made to ensure it found the exact matches. If an error occurred, which might signal a change in the data format, you print the error message to the screen:

```
if (count($matches) != 3) {
    // error - not the correct number of fields
    // this may signal a change to the format of the title field!
    print "Error: title '$title' isn't of the ➥
 format we're expecting\n";
    continue;
}
```

Now that you have the band and venue/date parsed, another **preg_match** is performed to separate the venue name from the date. You do it with the following regex:

```
preg_match("/^(.*)\s([\d]{1,2}\/[\d]{1,2})$/", ➥
 $venue_date, $venue_date_matches);
```

Again, let's take a look at that first argument, which is another regex pattern. Figure 3-4 displays the pattern, showing the parts of the regular expression that match the **venue** name and **date** fields.

Figure 3-4. Regular expression pattern used to match the venue name and date fields

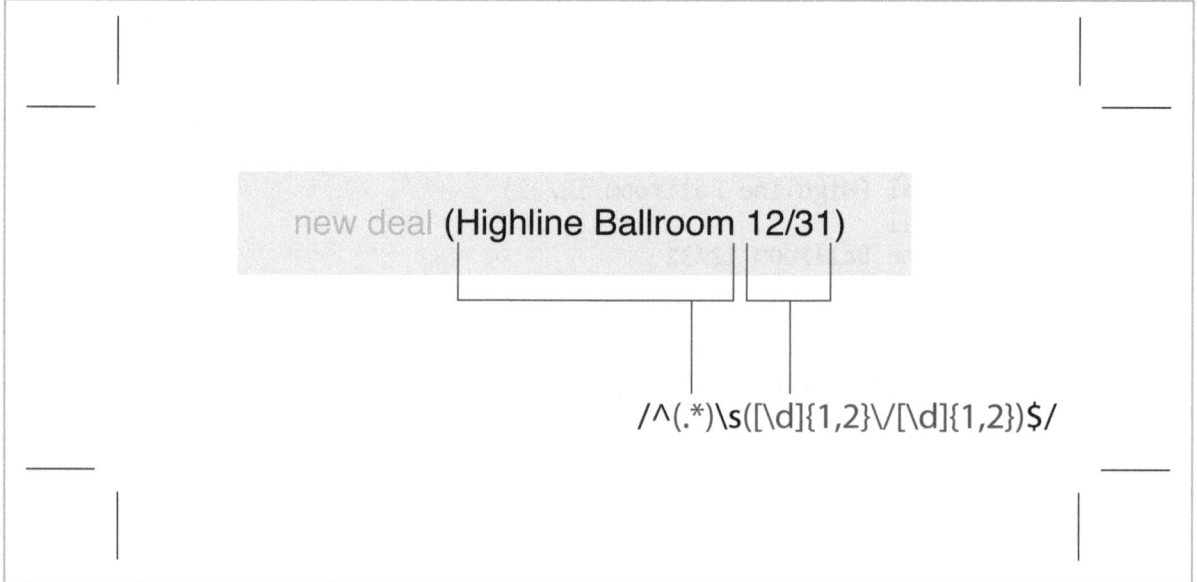

Once you run the string **$venue_date** through **preg_match**, the **$venue_date_matches** array will hold the subpatterns you specified in the regex and look like the following:

```
Array
(
    [0] => Highline Ballroom 12/31
    [1] => Highline Ballroom
    [2] => 12/31
)
```

You make another check to ensure the matches were found. If an error occurred, it could indicate a change in the format or that the month/date might be missing. In this case, you print a warning to the screen and continue, assuming that the date was missing:

```
if (count($venue_date_matches) == 3) {
    // parsing was successful
    $venue = $venue_date_matches[1];
    $date = $venue_date_matches[2];
} else {
    // venue/date were not in the format we were expecting but we'll move on
    // this could mean the date was missing or the format has changed!
    print "Warn: we didn't find the venue and ⇥
 date in '$venue_date'\n";
    $venue = $venue_date;
}
```

Finally, you print all the concert information that you just successfully parsed: band name, venue name, and concert date.

Nice job—you deserve a break after that one! But don't take long, because we're just getting into the good stuff.

Looking Up the Venue Location with Eventful's API

Now that you can parse the venue names from Tourfilter's feed, it's time to use the Eventful API to look up the location, specifically, the latitude and longitude of each venue.

Eventful provides APIs that allow you to search, create, and modify information in Eventful's events and venues database. Eventful provides a PHP library to use with its API, but you're going get your hands dirty and write your own library. Why do this? A few reasons. First, by writing the code yourself, you'll see what's happening "behind the scenes," which is basically retrieving and parsing the Eventful XML data. Second, the Eventful PHP library requires numerous PEAR libraries that you may not have available on your server.

Note   The PHP Extension and Application Repository (PEAR) contains numerous reusable PHP extensions and libraries. PEAR is typically installed alongside PHP, and most hosting companies have PEAR installed on their servers. Since you may not have PEAR installed on your server and the PEAR libraries don't provide much additional functionality for the examples, you won't be using PEAR in the examples in this book. You can find more information on PEAR at http://pear.php.net.

If, after reading this book, you continue to use Eventful's APIs for more than just searching for venue locations, you may want to use Eventful's PHP library because it handles authentication for some of the API calls. You can find more information about Eventful's API at http://api.eventful.com/docs.

In the following code, you'll create a simple PHP class that handles Eventful's venue search API call. Before you start writing the class, though, let's explore the venue search API to see how it is called and what it returns.

Eventful Venue Search API

According to the Eventful API documentation, the venue search API can be called with a simple HTTP GET request using a few search parameters. An HTTP GET request is what's performed when you type a URL into a browser and hit Return—the browser makes an HTTP request for a specified resource. You can call Eventful's APIs using the same approach.

When calling Eventful's venue search API, you must pass a few parameters to the API to indicate what you're searching for:

- **app_key** is the application key that Eventful assigns to you when you sign up for a developer account at **http://api.evdb.com**.

- **keywords** is the name of the venue you are searching, such as Knitting Factory.

- **location** is the city name, such as New York.

Using these parameters, you can construct a simple URL to call Eventful's venue search API. The following URL is an example of how to call the API, searching for the Knitting Factory in New York. Insert your own application key from Eventful in the following URL, and try opening the URL in a web browser: **http://api.evdb.com/rest/venues/search?app_key=your_api_key_goes_here&keyword s=Knitting+Factory&location=New+York**.

After opening the link in your browser, you should see XML output similar to Listing 3-6.

Listing 3-6. Sample XML

```
<?xml version="1.0" encoding="UTF-8"?>

<search version="0.2">
  <total_items>1</total_items>
  <page_size>10</page_size>
  <page_count>1</page_count>
  <page_number>1</page_number>
  <page_items>1</page_items>
  <first_item>1</first_item>
  <last_item>1</last_item>
  <search_time>0.031</search_time>
```

```
<venues>
    <venue id="V0-001-000444375-2">
    <name>The Knitting Factory</name>
    <venue_name>The Knitting Factory</venue_name>

    <description>Tel: (212) 219-3132
Fax: (212) 219-3401

Box Office Hours
Monday to Saturday: 10 AM until close
Sunday: 2 PM until close

Directions
You can take the 1 or 9 train to Franklin Street, ↪
 walk one block south to Leonard, turn left and walk a block &amp; ↪
a half to the club.

You can take the A, C or E train to Canal Street, ↪
 walk 4 blocks south and turn left on Leonard. ↪
 You could also take the N or R train to Canal Street, ↪
 walk down Broadway 4 blocks to Leonard, turn right, ↪
 and see the club at the far end of the block. ↪
 If you are unfamiliar with the downtown area ↪
click here for a full MTA New York City Subway Map</description>
    <venue_type>Concert Hall</venue_type>
    <address>74 Leonard Street</address>
    <city_name>New York</city_name>
    <region_name>New York</region_name>

    <region_abbr>NY</region_abbr>
    <postal_code>10013</postal_code>
    <country_name>United States</country_name>
    <country_abbr2>US</country_abbr2>
    <country_abbr>USA</country_abbr>
    <longitude>-74.005045</longitude>
    <latitude>40.717337</latitude>
    <geocode_type>EVDB Geocoder</geocode_type>
    <owner>evdb</owner>
    <timezone></timezone>
    <created></created>
    <event_count>108</event_count>
    <trackback_count>0</trackback_count>
```

```
      <comment_count>1</comment_count>
      <link_count>1</link_count>
      <image>
         <url>http://images.evdb.com/images/small/I0-001/000/422/864-9.jpg ↪
</url>
         <width>48</width>
         <height>48</height>
         <caption></caption>
      </image>
    </venue>
  </venues>
</search>
```

Examining the XML

The API returns a lot of useful information about the Knitting Factory: the address, a description, and even an image. Notice the latitude and longitude in the response—this is exactly what you need!

The search for the Knitting Factory worked pretty well for you. It returned a single result that matched the venue that you wanted. However, what if your search returned multiple results? How would you tell which is the proper venue? It would be easy to spot the correct venue by looking at it visually, but how do you handle this condition when you are automating the venue lookup? This is something you'll need to factor into your code.

If an invalid request is made to the Eventful API, an error response will be returned (see Listing 3-7). It's important to check for valid responses returned from the API call.

Listing 3-7. Sample Error XML from Eventful

```
<?xml version="1.0" encoding="UTF-8"?>
<error string="Authentication Error">
<description>The application key provided (abc123) is not registered with
EVDB. ↪
 A valid application key is required.</description>
</error>
```

Creating the Eventful Library

Now that you've seen what the API call and response both look like, it's time to build a library to handle the venue search functionality. Since you will be using only Eventful's venue search API at this time, you'll create a simple PHP class that contains a function called **searchVenue()**. This function will take a few arguments—a venue name, a location, and a search radius limit. The function will return the search results as a **SimpleXMLElement** object. It will be up to you to parse the SimpleXML results outside the class. You can find the Eventful PHP class in the file **Eventful.php**—take a look at the code in **Eventful.php** now, and I'll explain it in the following section.

Examining the Code

This class is very straightforward. Most of the work is done in the **get()** function, which builds the API URL, calls the API using CURL, and then returns the results as SimpleXML.

The **searchVenue()** function simply calls the **get()** function with the API method name **"venues/search"** and the search parameters.

The **get()** function creates the API URL that is requested using CURL. Remember from the previous example, the venue search API URL must contain a few parameters besides the method name: your application key, the venue name, and a location. You are also adding a couple optional parameters to the API call: **page_size** and **within** (search radius).

To construct the URL, each parameter is passed through the PHP function **urlencode()**, which ensures that the URL contains all valid characters. After constructing the URL, it should look something like this:

```
http://api.evdb.com/rest/venues/search?keywords=knitting+factory&location=↪
new+york&within=20&app_key=your_app_key_goes_here&page_size=5
```

Once the URL is created, the API is called, and the response from the API is converted into a **SimpleXMLElement** object. If the API call fails for any reason, **false** is returned. If this level of error checking isn't granular enough for you,

you can add code that checks the HTTP status code returned from CURL. I'll leave that as homework for you!

Using Your Eventful Library

Let's look at a quick example that uses the new Eventful library. The script **example_3_3_eventful_search.php** uses the Eventful library to search for the location of the Knitting Factory in New York.

Before running the script, remember to edit the code in **example_3_3_eventful_search.php** and specify your own app key in the variable **$app_key**.

Listing 3-8 shows the new script, **example_3_3_eventful_search.php**. Running the script will produce output similar to Listing 3-9. Go ahead and run the script now.

Listing 3-8. Using Eventful.php to Perform a Venue Search

```php
<?php

# Eventful Venue Lookup
# Requires SimpleXML (php5) and curl

header("Content-type: text/plain");

require ('Eventful.php');

$app_key = 'your app key goes here';
// create an instance of our Eventful library
$ev = new Eventful($app_key);

// create our search parameters
$params = array(
    'keywords' => "knitting factory",
    'location' => "new york",
    'within'   => 20,
);

// call the search API
$sxml = $ev->searchVenue($params);
```

```
// list the venues returned from the API
foreach ($sxml->venues->venue as $v) {
    print "venue name: " . $v->venue_name . "\n";
    print "latitude:   " . $v->latitude . "\n";
    print "longitude:  " . $v->longitude . "\n";
}

?>
```

Listing 3-9. Output from Search Script

```
venue name: The Knitting Factory
latitude:   40.717337
longitude:  -74.005045
```

Examining the Code

This is your first use of a PHP 5 class in this book. If you aren't familiar with how PHP 5 class and objects work, I recommend looking through the documentation at `http://us3.php.net/manual/en/language.oop5.basic.php`.

Using the `Eventful` class is simple. You create an `Eventful` object with the following code:

```
$ev = new Eventful($app_key);
```

This creates an `Eventful` object called `$ev`, which you can use to call the `searchVenue()` function. `searchVenue()` takes input parameters as an array, and you create the array in the example like this:

```
// create our search parameters
$params = array(
    'keywords' => "knitting factory",
    'location' => "new york",
    'within'   => 20,
);
```

You call `searchVenue()` with your parameters like this:

```
$sxml = $ev->searchVenue($params);
```

This example doesn't perform any error checking on the return value from your searchVenue() call—you'll add this in the next example. To print the venue name and latitude and longitude from your search, loop over the SimpleXML using the following:

```
foreach ($sxml->venues->venue as $v) {
    print "venue name: " . $v->venue_name . "\n";
    print "latitude:    " . $v->latitude . "\n";
    print "longitude:   " . $v->longitude . "\n";
}
```

Geocoding Tourfilter Data

Now that you can search for a venue's location using your Eventful library, it's time to combine the Eventful library with the previous examples so that you can look up the exact locations of the venues in Tourfilter's feed.

In the next example, the Eventful library has been added to code from the script **example_3_2_parse_tourfilter.php**, which was used to retrieve and parse Tourfilter's RSS feed. The updated script, **example_3_4_lookup_venues.php**, will be able to retrieve and parse all the data you need: band name, venue name, venue latitude/longitude, and concert date!

Before running the script **example_3_4_lookup_venues.php**, remember to edit the code to specify your own Eventful app key in the variable **$app_key**. Please note that the new script will take a while to run—anywhere from a minute or two! It takes this long because it retrieves the Tourfilter RSS feed and then makes a single API call to Eventful for each venue that it finds in the RSS feed. You'll learn about ways of speeding this up in the next chapter.

Examining the Code

Let's take a look at the changes made in the updated script: **example_3_4_lookup_venues.php**. First, you add the line **set_time_limit(0)** to the beginning of your script, which tells PHP not to limit the execution runtime of the script. Without this, the script might die before it has time to complete.

Next, you add your Eventful library to the code and call the **venueSearch()** function using the venue names that are parsed from the Tourfilter feed.

After making the venue search API call, some simple error checking is performed to make sure you received a proper response. In this example, you also verify that at least one venue was returned in the response.

Caution   In this example, you are assuming the first venue returned from Eventful is the correct one. This may not be the case, and you may assume an incorrect location for your venue.

Running the code produces output like that in Listing 3-10. Notice the error in the output? The search for the venue Sin-e in New York didn't produce any results. For now, you skip any concerts for which you can't find the venue latitude and longitude. If you don't have the latitude and longitude, you can't map it!

Listing 3-10. Output from Your Tourfilter + Eventful Code

```
title: Moe. (Highline Ballroom 1/1)
band:  Moe.
venue: Highline Ballroom
latitude: 40.7142
longitude: -74.0064
date:  1/1

title: john hollenbeck (Barbes 1/1)
band:  john hollenbeck
venue: Barbes
latitude: 40.66795
longitude: -73.983793
date:  1/1

Error: failed to retrieve location for venue Sin-e using parameters: ↪
 Sin-e,new york,20
```

```
title: Drazy Hoops (Living Room 1/1)
band:  Drazy Hoops
venue: Living Room
latitude: 40.721015
longitude: -73.98786
date:  1/1

title: Jenny Scheinman (Barbes 1/1)
band:  Jenny Scheinman
venue: Barbes
latitude: 40.66795
longitude: -73.983793
date:  1/1
```

Summary

At this point, you have now mastered the art of geocoding concert and venue data. Congrats! The first part of your mashup is in good shape, and in the next chapter you'll explore ways to expose your geocoded data to a Google Mapplet. After all, it's all about mapping the data, right? You will also learn how to speed up your geocoding script through caching.

Chapter 4: Creating Geocoded Data Feeds

In the previous chapter, you learned how to geocode Tourfilter's concert data. At this point in your mashup, you know the location of each concert in Tourfilter's feed. The next step in your mashup is to create a feed of the geocoded data and expose the data to your Google Mapplet.

You'll expand on the code you wrote in the previous chapter, finalizing the server-side portion of your mashup in this chapter. Over the next few pages, you will learn how to do the following:

- Create XML feeds of the geocoded Tourfilter data

- Add caching to speed up the geocoding process

- Use cron to automate the XML feed generation

Creating an XML Data Feed

To expose your geocoded data to a Mapplet, you will create an XML feed of the data that your Mapplet can access. The XML must be available on a public web server so that your Mapplet can grab the data.

In the last code example in Chapter 3, the venue location for each concert in Tourfilter's New York feed was output to the screen. In the next example, you'll modify that code so that it creates a simple XML file containing the geocoded concert data. The updated script, **example_4_1_output_venue_xml.php**, writes the Tourfilter concert data to an XML file on your web server. The format of the XML file is simple—containing the band name, venue name, concert date, and latitude/longitude for the venue.

Before running the updated script, create a new directory named **xml** in the same directory in which the script will run. Make sure the write permissions of the directory allow your web server write access to the directory. Run the script either from the command line or by calling the script via your browser. After running the script, the file **newyork.xml** will be created in the **xml** subdirectory. Listing 4-1 shows a sample of the geocoded XML format.

Listing 4-1. Truncated Example of newyork.xml

```
<?xml version="1.0" encoding="UTF-8"?>
<markers>
    <marker band="the black crowes" venue="Irving Plaza" date="3/4" ↪
lat="40.734725" lng="-73.988185" />
    <marker band="beastie boys" venue="Terminal 5" date="3/4" ↪
lat="40.769765" lng="-73.992192" />
</markers>
```

Examining the Code

The script **example_4_1_output_venue_xml.php** has been slightly modified to store all the venue information in the array **$xml** as it parses through the Tourfilter data and retrieves the venue information from Eventful. At the beginning of the script, you place the XML header and beginning **<markers>** tag in the **$xml** array:

```
$xml = array('<?xml version="1.0" encoding="UTF-8"?>');
$xml[] = '<markers>';
```

After you parse each concert in the Tourfilter feed, you create a marker for the concert. The marker holds the band name, venue name, concert date, latitude, and longitude. Then, you add each marker to your **$xml** array:

```
$xml[] = createMarkerXML($band, $venue, $date, ↪
(string)$v->latitude, (string)$v->longitude);
```

At the end of the script, you add the closing **<markers>** tag to your array and print the XML data to the file **newyork.xml**.

```
$xml[] = '</markers>';
```

Using Caching to Speed Up Your Geocoding

At this point, the geocoding script is pretty slow—it can take more than a minute to complete. And, just wait until you add more cities to it! Every time the script runs, it does a venue lookup using the Eventful web service for each venue in the Tourfilter feed. The venue information you need (latitude and longitude) may never change, so you can speed up the script's execution time by caching the venue's latitude and longitude locally on your own server. By storing the latitude and longitude data locally, you won't need to look it up at Eventful each time.

Caution   It is OK to cache Eventful's data for your application, but you must obtain permission from Eventful if you need to cache data for a commercial application using its services.

You have a few options when caching data from PHP programs. memcached (`http://www.danga.com/memcached`) and APC (`http://www.php.net/apc`) are two popular caching libraries for PHP. Other caching options are to store the data in a local database or in files on the file system. For simplicity sake, you'll write a simple file-caching class that will store all the venue location information in files on your local machine. If you are unfamiliar with caching, the concept is similar to a dictionary—you store key/value pairs in a cache, just like the word/definition pairs in a dictionary. The key is used to reference the data (or value) stored in the cache and should be unique. In this case, the data you will be storing in the cache is venue information (name, latitude, and longitude), and the cache "key" will contain the venue name and city. For each venue, you'll store a single key/value pair in the cache.

Here's what your caching logic will look like:

1. Parse the venue name from the Tourfilter feed.

2. See whether the venue exists in your local cache. If so, use it.

3. If the venue doesn't exist in the local cache, look it up at Eventful and store it in the cache.

To make sure the cache has a current copy of the data from Eventful, you will purge it daily. This will ensure that the data is less than a day old at most, and it will refresh itself with updated information from Eventful on a daily basis. The class will have a simple method to remove any data in the cache that is more than a day old and has thus "expired." The code in **SimpleCache.php** illustrates the simple caching class, called **SimpleCache**.

Examining the Code

The code in SimpleCache.php provides very basic caching functionality. This class has three main methods: **set**, **get**, and **flush**. The **flush** method will delete any files in the cache that are older than a specified time. The **get** method will retrieve data from the cache, and the **set** method will store data in the cache.

When storing data in the cache, the **serialize** function is used to convert the data (in this case, the venue information such as latitude and longitude) to a storable format. Once the data has been serialized, the data is stored in a file in the cache directory.

```php
function set($key, $var) {

    // get the cache file name
    $cache_file = $this->getCacheFileName($key);

    // serialize the venue object
    // and store it in our cache file
    $serialized_data = serialize($var);
    $fp = fopen($cache_file, "w");
    if (!$fp) {
        return false;
    }

    // write the serialized object to the file
    if (fwrite($fp, $serialized_data) === FALSE) {
        return false;
    }

    // close up the file
    fclose($fp);
    return true;
}
```

To retrieve data from the cache, you do just the opposite. The serialized data is read from the cache file and unserialized back into the original PHP data.

```php
function get($key) {
    $cache_file = $this->getCacheFileName($key);

    if (file_exists($cache_file)) {
        // let's read the object from the file
        $cache_data = file_get_contents($cache_file);
        $cache_object = unserialize($cache_data);

        // if the file_get_contents() or unserialize() failed,
        // $cache_object will have a value of false

        return $cache_object;
    } else {
        // we didn't find the cache file
        return false;
    }
}
```

Storing Venue Information in the Cache

Now that you have a caching library, I'll talk about the data that you will store in the cache. Remember that your goal is to speed up the geocode script. To do this, you need to limit the number of lookups you make using Eventful's venue search API. So, after each successful venue lookup is performed, the venue's latitude and longitude will be stored in the cache. Each time you run across the same venue, you can grab the latitude and longitude from the local cache, saving you a "trip" to Eventful for the information.

You can use a simple PHP class to store the venue information. Listing 4-3 shows the Venue class, which will hold the location, name, latitude, and longitude of a single venue. For each venue you find in the Tourfilter concert feeds, you'll create a Venue object, populate it with the venue data, and store it in the cache for later use.

Listing 4-3. Venue Class for Storing Basic Venue Information

```php
class Venue {
    // venue city
    public $location;
    // venue name
    public $name;
    // venue latitude
    public $latitude;
    // venue longitude
    public $longitude;

    public function __construct($location, $name, $lat, $lng) {
        $this->location = $location;
        $this->name = $name;
        $this->latitude = $lat;
        $this->longitude = $lng;
    }
}
```

Speeding Things Up

Let's apply the caching library and **Venue** class to your code in
example_4_1_output_venue_xml.php and watch the run time of your geocoding
script speed up. In the updated code,
example_4_2_output_venue_xml_with_cache.php, the **SimpleCache** and **Venue** classes
have been added to properly cache the venue location information.

Before running the script, make sure you have created the local cache directory
that will store all the cached data. The cache directory is specified in the
SimpleCache.php file and is **cache** by default. Make sure the cache directory you
use has the proper write permissions so that your web server can write to the
directory.

Once you have created the **cache** directory, run the script
example_4_2_output_venue_xml_with_cache.php. The script will take the same
amount of time to run as before, but it will store all venue information in the
local cache as it runs. After it completes, run the script a second time. Notice the

speed increase? Since you're storing the venue information on your local machine, the script run time should be cut drastically!

Examining the Code

The first addition to this script is to **require** the two new classes:

```
require ('SimpleCache.php');
require ('Venue.php');
```

Next, you create an instance of the new **SimpleCache** class. This is used to store and retrieve information from the cache.

```
$cache = new SimpleCache();
```

Before you start retrieving the data, you remove any old data from your cache with the **flush** method. The argument for the **flush** method is the amount of time you'd like for the files in the cache to stick around—24 hours in this case.

```
$cache->flush(60*60*24);
```

The rest the script remains unchanged, except for your caching additions. After the concert data is retrieved from Tourfilter, the script checks to see whether you have already stored any of the venue data in your local cache. All data in the cache is accessible by a cache "key." In this case, the cache "key" contains the city name and the venue name, separated by an underscore, as in **new york_Knitting Factory**. Checking the cache is simple; just pass the cache key to the method **get**, which will return the object that is found in the cache corresponding to that key or will return **FALSE** if it doesn't find anything. If the venue information is found in the cache, you use the latitude and longitude from the cache instead of looking it up at Eventful:

```
$cache_key = $location . "_" . $venue;
$v = $cache->get($cache_key);
if ($v !== FALSE) {
    // found the venue in the cache - create the XML for it
    $xml[] = createMarkerXML($band, $venue, $date, ↦
(string)$v->latitude, (string)$v->longitude);
    continue;
}
```

If you don't have a particular venue in your cache, you look it up using the Eventful API. After you successfully retrieve venue information from Eventful, you store the information in your cache using the **set** method. The **set** method takes two parameters: the cache key name and the data to cache. In this case, you are caching the **Venue** object.

```
$new_venue = new Venue($location, $venue, ↪
(string)$v->latitude, (string)$v->longitude);
$cache->set($cache_key, $new_venue);
```

Let's take a quick visual look at the caching logic to make sure it's clear. Figure 4-1 shows the caching logic the first time you try to find the latitude and longitude of the venue the Knitting Factory. The logic is simple. First, look for "Knitting Factory" in the cache. If it doesn't exist in the cache, search for the latitude and longitude of the venue at Eventful. Finally, take the latitude and longitude returned from Eventful and store it in your cache—you can use the information in the local cache the next time you need to look it up. Figure 4-1 demonstrates this.

Figure 4-2 shows the logic the next time you need to look up the Knitting Factory. As you did earlier, before searching for the latitude and longitude at Eventful, you look in your local cache first. Since you already have a copy stored, you'll use the copy from your cache.

Figure 4-1. Caching logic, looking up the Knitting Factory for the first time

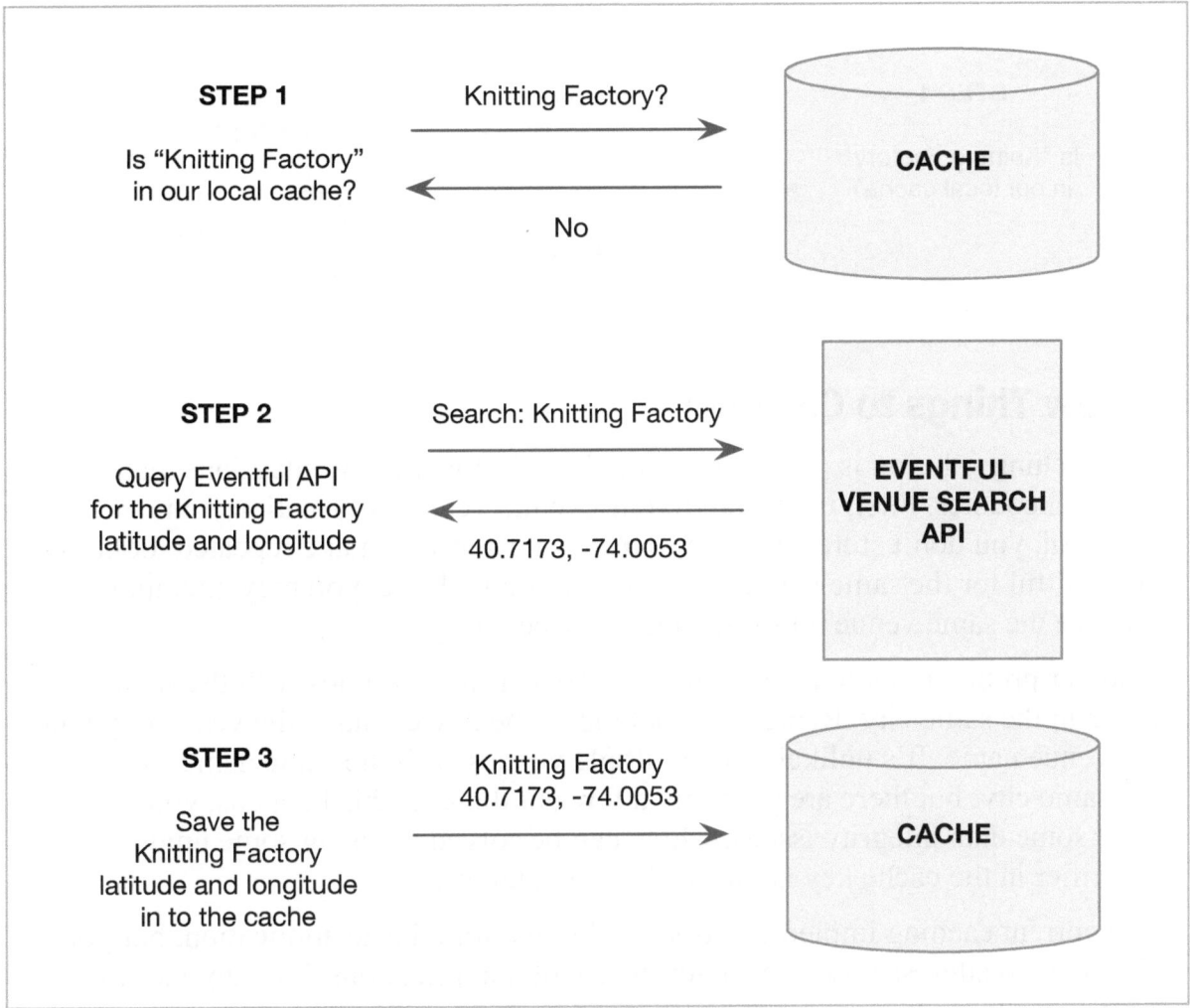

Figure 4-2. Caching logic, looking up the Knitting Factory the second time

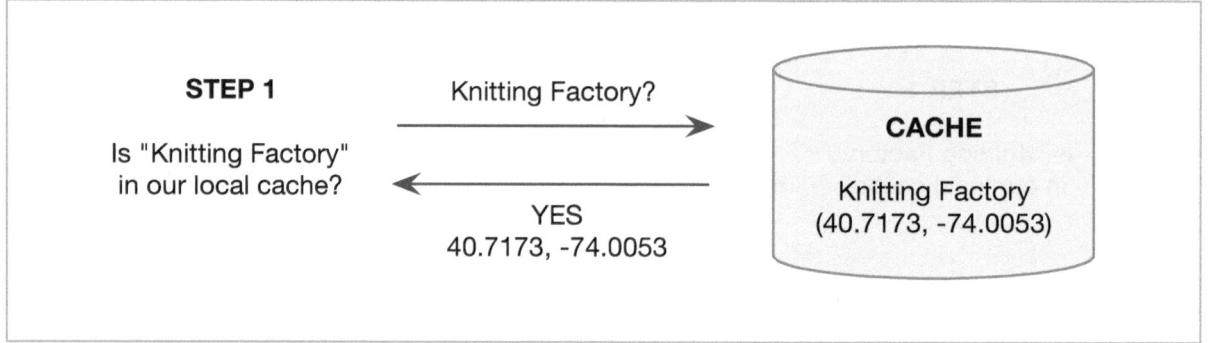

A Few Things to Consider

The caching solution is pretty basic and doesn't cover a few situations that you might encounter. First, if you fail to retrieve the venue information from Eventful, you don't store anything in the cache and will make repeated lookups at Eventful for the same venue. Without additional logic, you may attempt to retrieve the same venue multiple times unnecessarily.

Another problem that may arise involves two or more venues with the same name in the same city. Remember that the cache key contains the venue city and the venue name. It's unlikely that multiple venues with the same name exist in the same city, but there are probably a few out there. If this happens, you will have some data integrity issues, which can be solved by using some unique identifier in the cache key name, such as an address.

The current caching implementation works fine for a basic application, but you will need to address these issues for production applications. Did anyone say homework?

Adding More Cities!

All the previous examples in this book have involved retrieving concert listings for New York only. Some of you might be saying, "Well, why would you need anything else?" but let's make the mashup more compelling by retrieving listings for other cities as well. Tourfilter currently has listings for nearly 60 cities, so let's modify the script to retrieve data for all of them!

Updating your code to accommodate Tourfilter's entire list of cities is pretty easy. You add an array that contains the list of cities that your script will retrieve to the beginning of the script. You could move this to a configuration file, but leaving it in the script makes it more readable.

example_4_3_output_venue_xml.php includes all cities currently on Tourfilter's site. The code has been modified slightly to retrieve the data for each city. Now that you are retrieving the data for nearly 60 cities, the script will take a while to run! Try running the script now. Once the script is done, you will have a geocoded XML file for each city in the xml directory.

Examining the Code

You'll notice the $cities array near the top of the script. This array contains a few fields of information for each city: location, xml file name, and url. The location field contains the city and state or city and country name. The xml_file_name field holds the name of the file that will contain the geocoded XML data for the city. And, finally, the url field contains the URL for the concert data at tourfilter.com.

```
$cities = array(
    array (
        "location" => "new york, ny",
        "xml_file_name" => "newyork",
        "url" => "http://www.tourfilter.com/newyork/rss/by_concert_date",
    ),
    array (
        "location" => "albuquerque, nm",
        "xml_file_name" => "albuquerque",
        "url" =>
"http://www.tourfilter.com/albuquerque/rss/by_concert_date",
    ),
);
```

Finally, you add a simple foreach loop around your previous script, looping over each city in the $cities array and retrieving the data for each city:

```
foreach ($cities as $city) {

        $location = $city["location"];
        $url = $city["url"];
        $xml_file_name = $city["xml_file_name"];
```

Automating the Script Using cron

Now that your script is finally in place, you can set it up to run every hour automatically. You can do this using cron, which is a Unix-based scheduling tool. If you are on a non-Unix platform, you can use a similar scheduling program for your operating system.

cron can be tricky to set up if you've never done it before, but no fear. There are a few options for configuring cron, and I'll show you how to do it from the command line. If you are running your code on a hosted web server, your hosting company will typically offer a web-based configuration tool for cron.

To schedule the script to run hourly, you will need to edit your crontab file, which contains your list of scheduled tasks. The following shows how to schedule the latest script to run once every hour:

1. Edit the crontab file by typing **crontab -e** at the command line (shell). If you don't have any tasks previously scheduled, this command will open an empty file.

2. Add the following line to your crontab file, editing the directory to match the directory on your server where your updated script resides. Please note that I've renamed the script **example_4_3_output_venue_xml.php** to **tourfilter.php**:

   `0 * * * * cd /path/to/your/directory/; php tourfilter.php`

3. Save the file and quit.

   In this example, the script **tourfilter.php** should run at the top of each hour of each day. Following the fields that specify the schedule, you tell cron to first **cd** to the directory that contains your script (make sure you change this to reflect your directory name!) and then run your script (which you've renamed **tourfilter.php**).

Before moving on, let's take a look at the line you added to the crontab file and what each field means:

```
0 * * * * cd /path/to/your/directory/; php tourfilter.php
```

The first five fields of the line specify when the script should run:

- The first field specifies the minutes of the hour when the script should run, from 0 to 59. In this example, it will run at the top of each hour.

- The second field specifies which hour or hours that the script should run, from 0 to 23. The * in this example means it will run every hour.

- The third field specifies the day of the month, from 1 through 31. The * in this example means it will run every day.

- The fourth field specifies the month, from 1 through 12. The * in this example means it will run every month.

- The fifth field specifies the day of the week, from 0 through 6, where 0 is Sunday. The * in this example means it will run every day.

Note   Jobs scheduled by cron typically run scripts as another user. Make sure the permissions of your **cache** and **xml** directories are set so the cron user can write to the directories. You can use the following commands on Unix-based file systems to grant all users all rights to the **cache** and **xml** directories:

```
chmod -R a+rwx cache/*
```

```
chmod -R a+rwx xml/*
```

You can set up cron to e-mail or log any output that the script generates. The script currently contains multiple **print** statements that output useful debugging information. The following shows a few ways to use cron to gather the script output (or just ignore it!):

- To have the output e-mailed to you each time the script runs, use the following lines in your crontab file:

```
MAILTO=your_email_address
0 * * * * cd /path/to/your/directory/; php tourfilter.php
```

- To have the output written to a log file instead of being e-mailed to you, try the following:

```
0 * * * * cd /path/to/your/directory/; ↵
php tourfilter.php >> /tmp/tfilter.log
```

- And, finally, to ignore all the output generated to the script, use the following:

```
0 * * * * cd /path/to/your/directory/; ↵
php tourfilter.php >> /dev/null 2>&1
```

Summary

Congratulations—the server portion of the mashup is complete! In the next chapter, you will finalize your mashup by completing the Mapplet. The Mapplet will display all the great content you are now geocoding. It's almost time to sit back and watch all of the bands coming through your city. You're almost there. One more chapter to go!

Chapter 5: Finalizing the Mashup

OK, you are finally here. You have the Mapplets API basics down and have a nice set of geocoded Tourfilter and Eventful data ready to be mapped. In the previous chapter, you finalized the server-side portion of your mashup, and now it's time to build the Mapplet.

Using some of the code you wrote in Chapter 2, you will build a Mapplet to retrieve and map the concert and venue data you've geocoded over the past few chapters. In this chapter, you'll put the finishing touches on your mashup, learning how to do the following:

- Retrieve the geocoded Toufilter data from your Mapplet

- Display concert data for all 60 cities in your geocoded data feed

- Style your Mapplet with basic HTML and CSS

- Install your Mapplet and share it with others

Displaying the Geocoded Data on a Mapplet

In the previous chapter, you created geocoded feeds of Tourfilter's concert data. If you set up the geocoding script from the previous chapter to run as a cron job, you should have a geocoded XML file for multiple cities sitting on your server (updated hourly). Now that you have this data ready, it's time to build the Google Mapplet to display all of this great data on a map.

Note   The Mapplet you are building in this chapter needs to access the geocoded XML data on a public web server. Make sure that the XML data files are publicly available on your server, such as at
`http://yourserver.com/mashup/data/newyork.xml`.

Chapter 2 left you with some Mapplet code that retrieved XML data from a web server and displayed the data on a map. Let's modify that code to retrieve one of the geocoded Tourfilter feeds, starting with New York, and display the concert data on a map. You'll add the rest of the cities later in the chapter.

Planning the Mapplet

What should your Mapplet look like? What should the interaction be? Let's keep it clean and simple and first take a look at the data that you have to work with so that you can plan what it's going to look like. From the geocoded XML file for concerts in New York, `newyork.xml`, you have the following information for each concert:

- Band name
- Venue name
- Concert date
- Venue latitude
- Venue longitude

On the map, you'll display a marker for each concert, with the marker placed on the map using the venue's latitude and longitude. Each marker will display an info window when clicked. The info window will contain the band name, venue name, and date of the show.

In the left panel of the Mapplet, you'll display the full list of the band and venue names. The user should be able to "drive" the map from the list, so the band names will be clickable—displaying the info window for that particular concert. I'll leave the CSS styling out of this example and show how to add that later in the chapter.

1. Open the Mapplet Scratch Pad in your browser at `http://maps.google.com/maps/mm`.

2. Edit the Mapplet source in `example_5_1_map_concert_data.xml`, and make sure the URL in the following line points to your server and directory that contains the geocoded XML:

   ```
   var url = "http://yourserver.com/path/to/xml/" + city + ".xml";
   ```

3. After editing **example_5_1_map_concert_data.xml**, copy and paste the contents of the file into the Mapplet Scratch Pad.

4. Click the Preview button in the scratch pad. You should see a Mapplet similar to that shown in Figure 5-1.

5. Once the Mapplet loads, click the Load Data link to load the New York concert data.

Figure 5-1. New York concert data displayed in your Mapplet

Examining the Code

The Mapplet **example_5_1_map_concert_data.xml** is an updated version of your Mapplet from Chapter 2. You've modified it to retrieve the New York Tourfilter concert data that you've geocoded, display the list of concerts in the left panel of your Mapplet, and plot each of the concerts on the map. Let's take a look through the highlights of the Mapplet code.

First, since you may have a long list of concerts to display in the left panel of your Mapplet, you'll need to resize the height of the panel to accommodate the size of the list dynamically. You can accomplish this by adding the **dynamic-height** option to your Mapplet preferences in the header of the Mapplet:

```
<Require feature="dynamic-height" />
```

Calling the **_IG_AdjustIFrameHeight()** function after you retrieve the XML data and render the list of concerts will resize the left panel properly.

The next change you've made is to the **loadData** function, which now takes a city name as an argument. The city name is used in the URL where you fetch the geocoded XML data.

```
function loadData(city) {

    var url = "http://yourserver.com/path/to/xml/" + city + ".xml";

    // ...
```

After constructing the URL using the city name, **_IG_FetchXmlContent()** fetches the New York XML file from your server. Once the XML file is retrieved, the function **handleFetchContent()** is called with the XML passed as an argument, You've gotten a little fancy here by adding the **_IG_Callback()** wrapper, which allows you to pass additional parameters to a callback function. In this case, it means you want to pass the city name along with the XML data that was fetched to **handleFetchContent()**. The following code illustrates this:

```
// fetch the XML data from the url
_IG_FetchXmlContent(url, _IG_Callback(handleFetchContent, city));
```

Inside `handleFetchContent()`, some error checking is done on the retrieved data (the New York XML file) before the data is parsed. Most of the work takes place in the **for** loop, where a marker is placed on the map for each concert and where the HTML for the left panel, displaying the list of concerts, is built:

```
for (var i = 0; i < concertData.length; i++) {
    var concert = concertData[i];

    var band  = concert.getAttribute("band");
    var venue = concert.getAttribute("venue");
    var date  = concert.getAttribute("date");
    var lat   = concert.getAttribute("lat");
    var lng   = concert.getAttribute("lng");

    // create a marker and add it to the map
    var point = new GLatLng(lat, lng);
    var marker = createMarker(point, city, band, venue, date);
    map.addOverlay(marker);

    // add marker to your array so that you can track them
    markers[i] = marker;

    // add the point to your Bounds object
    bounds.extend(point);

    if (date != displayDate) {
        displayHTML += "<div class='date'>" + date + "</div>";
        displayDate = date;
    }

    displayHTML += "<div class='listing'>";
    displayHTML += " <a href='#' onclick='clickMarker(" + i + ");'>" + ↪
band + "</a>";
    displayHTML += " <span class='venue'>" + venue + "</span>";
    displayHTML += "</div>";
}
```

Adding the Full List of Cities

The Mapplet works nicely for a single city, so let's add support for all the cities in the geocoded Tourfilter feed. The **loadData()** function in the Mapplet takes a city name as an argument, so adding support for the rest of the cities will be easy. Since there are quite a few cities in the feed (about 60), you'll add a simple selection list to allow users to choose the city's concerts to view.

1. As in the previous example, edit the Mapplet source in **example_5_2_map_concert_data.xml**, and make sure the URL in the following line points to your server and directory that contains the geocoded XML:

    ```
    var url = "http://yourserver.com/path/to/xml/" + city + ".xml";
    ```

2. After editing **example_5_2_map_concert_data.xml**, copy and paste the contents of the file into the Mapplet Scratch Pad.

3. Click the Preview button in the scratch pad.

4. Once the Mapplet loads, select any of the cities in the selection list to view the concerts for that city. The Mapplet in Figure 5-2 shows a view of concerts for Portland, Oregon.

Figure 5-2. Viewing concert data for Portland, Oregon

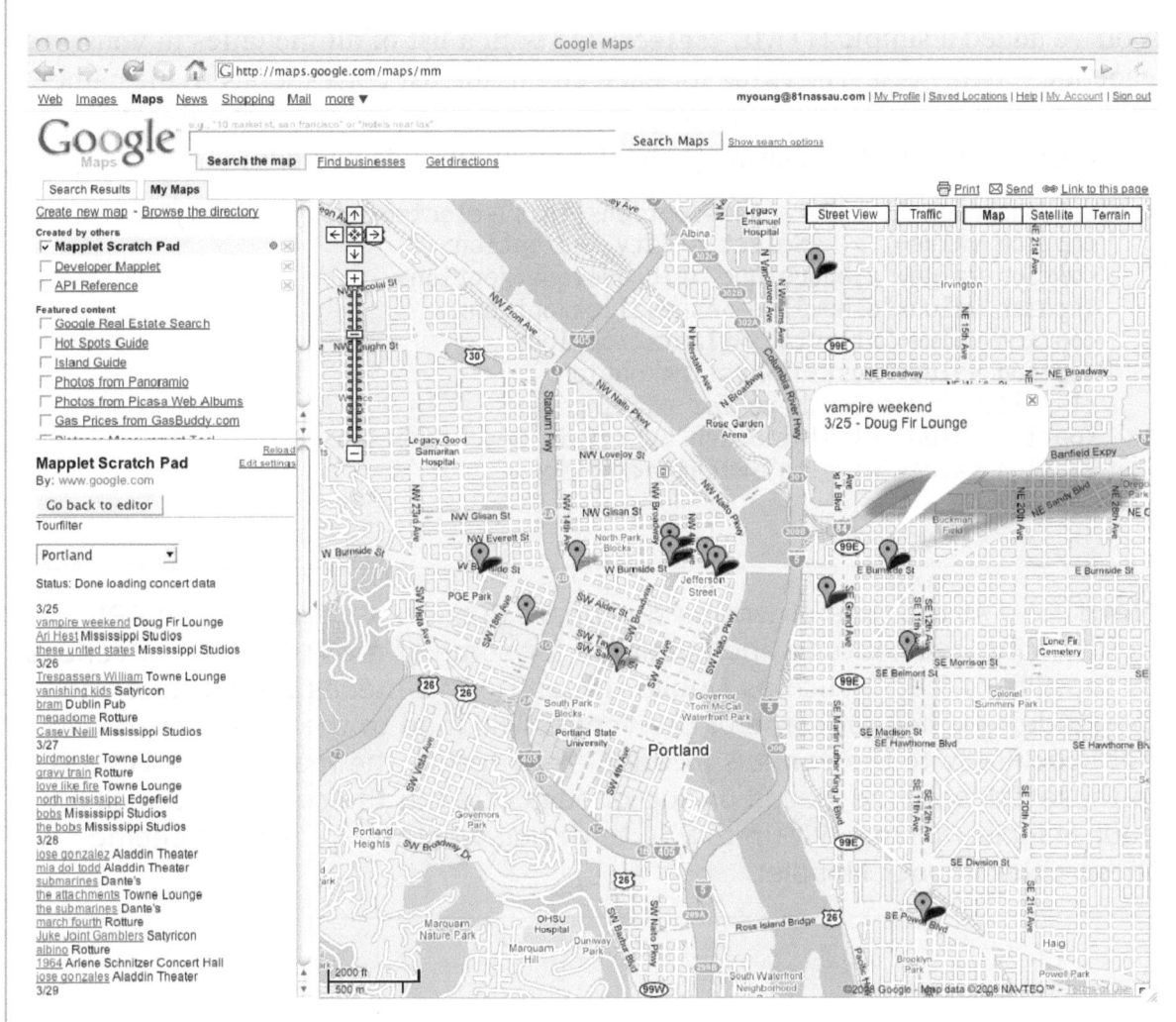

Examining the Code

You've added a simple HTML **<select>** tag with a list of all the cities in your geocoded XML feed. The **value** for each city in the list corresponds to the name of the XML file sitting on your server. When a city is selected in the list, the **onchange** event calls the **loadData()** function with the selected city:

```
<select onchange="loadData(this.options[this.selectedIndex].value);">
    <option value="">-- Select a City --</option>
    <option value="albuquerque">Albuquerque</option>
    <option value="asheville">Asheville</option>
    <option value="atlanta">Atlanta</option>
    <option value="austin">Austin</option>
    <!-- list truncated here for viewing -->
    <option value="virginiabeach">Virginia Beach</option>
    <option value="wichita">Wichita</option>
</select>
```

Note   At the time of writing this book, Eventful's venue search API returns city-level latitude and longitude for some of the international venues in Tourfilter's feeds (such as Dublin, Ireland). This means the latitude and longitude returned for some of the venues will map to the center of the city, not specifically to the venue's location. As a result, the markers for venues in these cities will be placed on top of each other in the center of the city in your Mapplet. I'll leave it up to you to decide whether it's worth keeping these cities in your Mapplet.

Styling the Mapplet

The Mapplet is now displaying the geocoded data for 60 cities! It's very functional at this point, but it's not really pretty. I've left the styling to the end, but the time has come to add some HTML and CSS to make your Mapplet a little easier on the eyes.

In the next (and final!) example, let's add some basic CSS to give the Mapplet a similar look and feel to tourfilter.com. You will add some simple CSS to style the left panel of the Mapplet, which contains the list of concerts for each city. The look and feel of the info windows needs improving too, so you'll add some inline CSS (meaning it's embedded in the HTML). Finally, you'll add a link to the event information page on tourfilter.com to each info window as well.

`example_5_3_map_concert_data.xml` contains the updated code. You know the drill at this point—edit the URL of the data feed in `example_5_3_map_concert_data.xml` to point to your server, and drop the updated code into the Mapplet Scratch Pad. Figure 5-3 shows the updated Mapplet, with the new and improved look.

Figure 5-3. Your Mapplet after some basic HTML/CSS additions

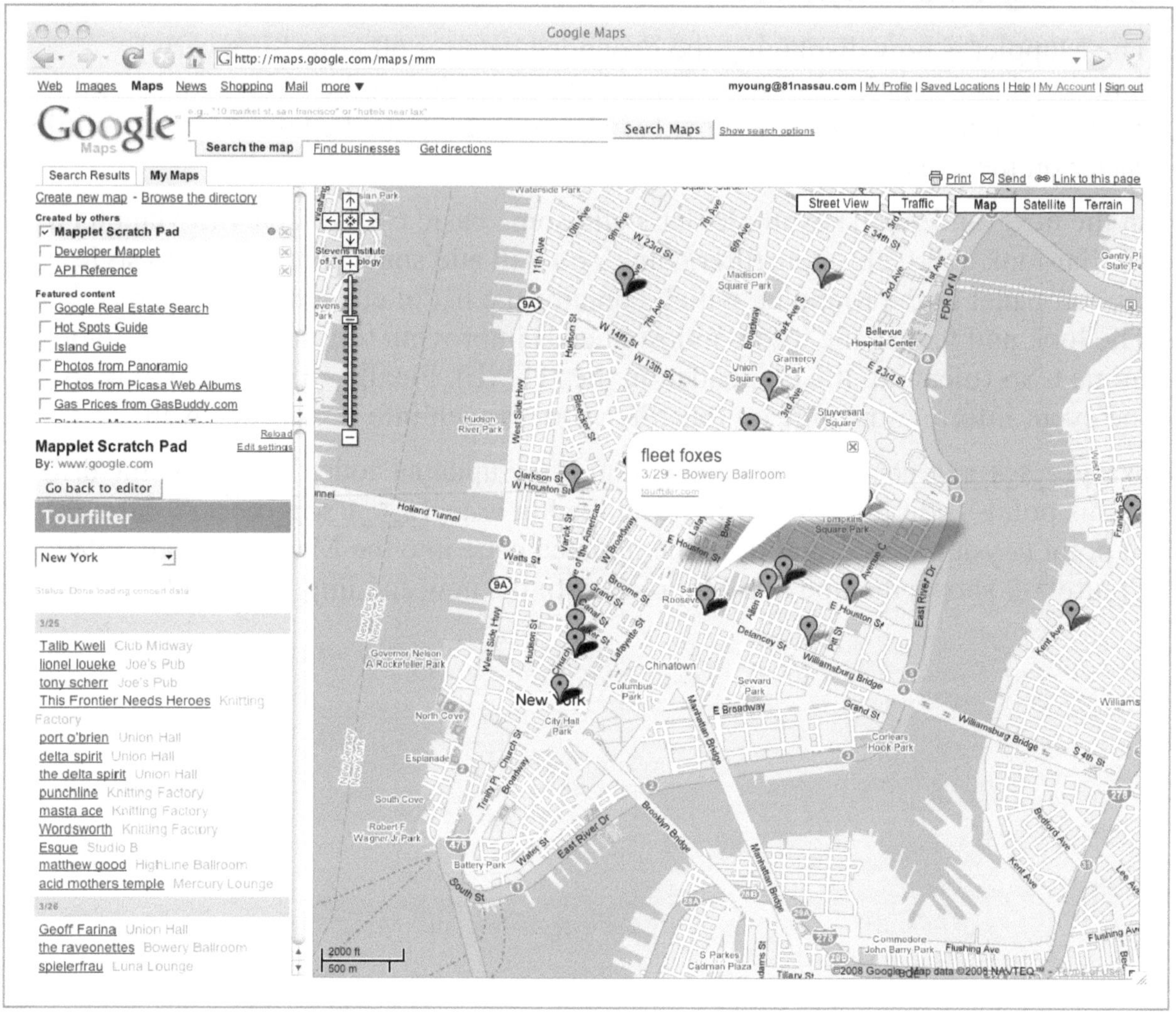

Examining the Code

You made simple additions to **example_5_3_map_concert_data.xml** to help add some basic styling to it. You added CSS to update the look of the components in the left panel of the Mapplet: the header, dates, band, and venue names.

Next, you updated the **createMarker()** function to include CSS in each of the concert info windows: first, the band name:

```
var html = "<div>";
html += " <span style='font-size: 18px; color: #900'>" +  band + "</span> ";
html += "</div>";
```

followed by the date and venue name:

```
html += "<div>";
html += " <span style='font-size: 14px; color: #888'>" + date + " - </span>";
html += " <span style='margin-top: 5px; font-size: 14px; color: #888'>" + ↪
 venue + "</span>";
html += "</div>";
```

and, finally, a link to the concert information page at tourfilter.com:

```
html += "<div style='margin-top: 5px; font-size: 10px; color: #888'>";
html += " <a style='color: #888;' href='" + tourfilter_url + "' ↪
 target='_blank'> tourftiler.com</a>"
html += "</div>";
```

Installing Your Mapplet

You've run all the Mapplet examples in this book from the Mapplet Scratch Pad.
Now that your Mapplet has some polish to it, it's time to move it from the
scratch pad to its own, much-deserved home.

It's quite easy to install a Mapplet. First, you need to make sure the final
Mapplet, example_5_3_map_concert_data.xml, is accessible on a public web server.
I recommend renaming it to something more suitable, such as
tourfilter_mapplet.xml. After you've made sure it's on your web server, go to
the Google Mapplet directory in your browser—you can get there by clicking the
"Browse the directory" link on your Google Maps page or from the following
link: http://maps.google.com/ig/directory?synd=mpl&pid=mpl&features=sharedmap,
geofeed.

Once you are in the Mapplet directory, click the Add by URL link, paste your
Mapplet URL into the input box, and click Add. Clicking Back to Google Maps
should take you back to your Mapplet list, with your new Tourfilter Concerts
Mapplet in the list. Click the Mapplet and explore!

Sharing Your Mapplet

If you want to share your work of art (your Mapplet) with others, you have a few options. Google will automatically create both a preview page and an install page for your Mapplet, and sharing both of these pages is quite simple.

Mapplet Preview Page

To create a preview page of your Mapplet, use the following URL: `http://maps.google.com/maps/mpl?moduleurl=http://yourserver.com/path/to/your/mapplet.xml`. Make sure you replace the `moduleurl` with the URL of your Mapplet!

You can e-mail this link or embed it into a web page. Users who click the link will be taken to a preview page of your Mapplet. The preview page includes a Save to My Maps link that allows users to add your Mapplet to their own Google Maps page.

Mapplet Install Page

To create a page that allows users to install your Mapplet, use the following URL: `http://maps.google.com/ig/add?synd=mpl&pid=mpl&moduleurl=http://yourserver.com/path/to/your/mapplet.xml`. Again, make sure you replace the `moduleurl` with the URL of your Mapplet!

This URL can also be embedded into a web page or e-mailed to your friends and users. Anyone who clicks the link will be prompted to install your Mapplet on their own Google Maps page.

Notice when you install the Mapplet via this URL, the install page includes space for a screenshot of your Mapplet. Figure 5-4 shows a Mapplet install page; the big white box next to your Mapplet name is where a screenshot should be. Your install page isn't very enticing without a screenshot of your Mapplet, so I encourage you to create one for your own Mapplet! You can find more information on how to create a custom screenshot for your Mapplet, as well as all the information you need on publishing your Mapplet, here: `http://code.google.com/apis/gadgets/docs/publish.html`.

Figure 5-4. Your Mapplet install page (without preview screenshot)

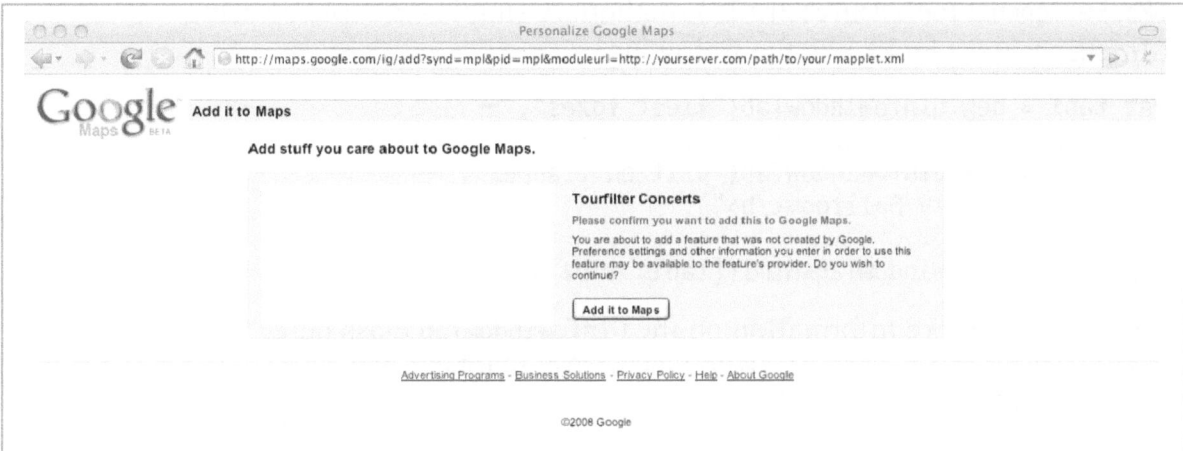

Next Steps

Congratulations! You have just built a full-fledged geographic mashup using a data source (Tourfilter), a web service (Eventful), and Google Mapplets. So, what's next? Well, you could make a few improvements to the mashup you just completed. I have a few suggestions for continuing with what you've built so far in this book.

Multiple Markers in Same Location

You may have noticed in your mashup that markers for the same concert get placed on top of each other so that only one of the markers is clickable. The user is able to view each of the markers by clicking the band name in the concert list in the left panel of your Mapplet, but not from the map. This is a common problem with map-based mashups—how do you handle data that needs to be mapped at the same latitude and longitude? One way of handling this is to display information about each of the concerts that happen at the same venue in a single info window.

Another way to handle this is to use info window tabs via the `GInfoWindowTab` class, which allows you to display multiple info windows in a tabbed interface above a marker in your Mapplet. Create a `GInfoWindowTab` object for each concert played at the same venue, and then pass each of those objects to the `GMarker.openInfoWindowTabsHtml()` method. A simple example of using `GInfoWindowTab`s looks like the following:

```
var tab1 = new GInfoWindowTab("fleet foxes", →
"<b>3/29 - Bowery Ballroom</b>");
var tab2 = new GInfoWindowTab("blitzen trapper", →
"<b>3/29 - Bowery Ballroom</b>");

marker.openInfoWindowTabsHtml([tab1, tab2]);
```

You can find more information on the `GInfoWindowTab` class here: `http://code.google.com/apis/maps/documentation/mapplets/reference.html#GInfoWindowTab`.

User Preferences in Mapplets

Google Mapplets (and Gadgets) let you store user preferences. One nice addition to the Tourfilter Mapplet would be to store the user's local city or city of choice. Once you've stored this, the Mapplet can load the user's favorite city each time they visit the Mapplet. This saves the user from having to select their city out of the list each time!

You can find more information on storing user preferences, including a simple example, here: `http://code.google.com/apis/maps/documentation/mapplets/services.html#Storing_User_Preferences`.

GeoRSS and KML

In Chapter 4, you created a geocoded feed of Tourfilter's data using a simple XML format. You can extend the same code to output the data as GeoRSS or KML: two location-based XML schemas.

You can use KML to display geographic data within Google Earth, Google Maps, and even Google Maps for Mobile! How great would it be to get a list of nearby concerts on your phone while you're out and about on a Saturday night? You can find more information on KML at `http://code.google.com/apis/kml/documentation/`.

GeoRSS, which basically means putting location data within RSS or Atom feeds, gives your users access to your content and geographic metadata. Exposing your geographic metadata with GeoRSS lets your users, and possibly savvy developers, build interesting ways to explore your data, just as you did with Tourfilter's data.

Another benefit of GeoRSS is that data in this format can be easily imported directly into Google Maps, Google Earth, Yahoo Maps, and Microsoft Virtual Earth.

Build Your Own!

Come on, I'm sure you have an idea for your own mashup, right? Take what you've learned from this book, and apply it to the data set that you want to map. You have the tools. It's time to roll up the sleeves and get coding!

Submitting Your Mapplet to the Google Directory

Once you build your own Mapplet, make sure you submit it to the Google Mapplet directory. This will help give exposure to your Mapplet, letting Google Maps users easily install and enjoy your hard work.

Summary

Well, that's the end of your journey! I hope it has been enjoyable and you've learned a thing or two about geographic mashups along the way. It's time now to take your mashup idea and apply the knowledge from this book to create a great new mashup—or, at least one to help me find a good happy-hour spot after work!

Copyright

Google Maps Mashups with Google Mapplets

© 2008 by Michael Young

ISBN-13 (electronic): 978-1-4302-0996-6

ISBN-13 (paperback): 978-1-4302-0995-9

Distributed to the book trade in the United States by Springer-Verlag New York, Inc., 233 Spring Street, 6th Floor, New York, NY 10013, and outside the United States by Springer-Verlag GmbH & Co. KG, Tiergartenstr. 17, 69112 Heidelberg, Germany.

In the United States: phone 1-800-SPRINGER, fax 201-348-4505, e-mail orders@springer-ny.com, or visit http://www.springer-ny.com. Outside the United States: fax +49 6221 345229, e-mail orders@springer.de, or visit http://www.springer.de.

For information on translations, please contact Apress directly at 2855 Telegraph Ave, Suite 600, Berkeley, CA 94705. Phone 510-549-5930, fax 510-549-5939, e-mail info@apress.com, or visit http://www.apress.com.